Crappie Fishing
Secrets and Tips of a Game Warden

by
Wayne Eller

Copyright 1986 by Wayne Eller
All Rights reserved

Library of Congress Catlog Card Number: 86-91856

Eller, Wayne

Crappie Fishing Secrets And Tips Of A Game Warden

xxxx xxxx xxxx

Printed in the United States of America by Viking Press Inc., Minneapolis, Minnesota.

Composition by Graphics Unlimited Inc.

Book Design by Bruce Harrington

All rights reserved. No part of this publication may be reproduced or used in any form or by any means - graphic, electronic, or mechanical, including photocoping, recording, taping, or stored in a data base or retrieval system without written permission of the publisher.

Front cover photo by Wayne Eller

Back cover photo by Joel Stedman

Published by Wayne Eller
144 South Shore Drive
Forest Lake, Minnesota 55025

ACKNOWLEDGEMENTS

There are so many people to thank for helping make this book possible. First of all, I am grateful for the devotion of my family, Nancy, Stanley, Lisa, Charles, and David who have encouraged me every step of the way.

Next I would like to thank the sportsmen and sportswomen that are both a part of my day to day contacts and the many new thoughtful acquaintances along the way for their ideas and generousity. Notably a special thanks to Mr. Eugene Swinson of Micanopy, Florida. After finding me with a busted down boat trailer over a thousand miles from my home, Mr. Swinson, a fellow angler that I had not known before, welded the trailer back together and got me under way, just to be a good samaritan.

I wish to thank Minnesota Conservation Officer Kermit Piper for sharing his ideas and tips on photography. And I have learned much about fishing from Officers Piper, David Olsen, Mike Kuhn, and Gary Thell through our camaraderie in our many hours of fishing together. Thanks also to Officers Reid Alter, Steve Jacobson, and David Rodahl for their contributions.

Finally, thanks to Lorraine Eitel of Bethel College, in St. Paul, Minnesota and John Daily of the fisheries division of the Minnesota Department Of Natural Resources for their assistance in editing this book.

TABLE OF CONTENTS

                                                          Page

1. **So this is a crappie** 1
   An introduction to the two types of crappies, comparing their basic differences, where they are found, and what types of conditions such as weather, temperatures, and other physical factors influence successful angling.

2. **The secret of the marabou jig** 13
   The best crappie lure design, including the most effective weight, length, material, and colors based on biological responses and habitat. And the effectiveness of the lure on other fish.

3. **Making and using the marabou jig** 26
   Four easy steps to making crappie jigs, excellent colors for special situations, and the proper techniques for presenting the lure to the fish.

4. **Give 'em enough line and they'll hang themselves** 39
   The proper care and best weight of fishing line. Tips for playing and landing big crappies. The most effective type of crappie rods and reels.

5. **From bobber to basket** 49
   A discussion on the use of a variety of equipment to improve crappie-fishing techniques.

6. **"Look out below, crappies!"** 56
   General procedures for locating crappies. Specific methods on when and how to fish ice out or late-winter crappies in canals, bays, and flowing water situations.

7. **Undercover crappies and other shallow shady secrets** 66
   Finding crappies under floating cattail bogs, water hyacinths, and other shaded structures. The three best patterns for fishing "reeds."

8. **They're in the trees!** 77
   How to find and fish for crappies in flooded timber from small ponds to reservoirs, including beaver lodges, cypress tree roots, and creek channels. How to locate timber spawning areas.

9. **Cabbage patch fish and the summer school gang** 90
   How to locate a crappie's favorite aquatic plants, when and where crappies go after spawning and during the summer. Fishing pondweeds, weed lines, drop offs, humps, points, suspended fish, summer darkness, and insect hatches.

10. River crappies: "Beside still waters" 101
   Where to find crappies in rivers and streams. Finding eddies (where crappies and other fish rest and feed) which are created by peninsulas, timber, bridge pilings, islands, boulders, river bends, and tail waters.

11. Crappies through the ice 111
   How to find crappie sanctuaries through the ice. Using a slip bobber and other winter equipment. The best time of day and bait for winter fishing.

12. Conservation: a call to stewardship 120
   A discussion of why some people violate fish and game laws using actual cases to illustrate the problems conservation officials encounter. What happens to confiscated fish and equipment. Other types of conservation problems.

Appendix A   Finding supplies for making jigs 133

Appendix B   How to build a fly tying vise 134

Appendix C   Making a marker buoy 135

Introduction

When I meet anglers during my day-to-day work as a wildlife officer, I like to put them at ease by visiting a few minutes before asking them for their licenses. And I usually ask them what they are fishing for. Many will answer, "Anything that bites." I am always impressed with someone who responds, "Crappies!" or another who might answer, "Walleyes!" or yet another who confidently answers,"Bass." Such self-assured responses usually comes from experienced anglers who know exactly what they are doing.

Fishing at its best is a well-developed art form. And those who are good at it are most assuredly artists. It takes years of hard work and commitment to become an excellent angler; neither luck nor accident has much to do with it. Trial and error does play an important role in developing angling skills. But not everyone need go through all the trials and errors. Novices and veterans alike can greatly benefit by reading, observing, questioning, and, yes, even sharing their "how to" ideas and secrets. There are, however, very few shortcuts to good fishing.

When I first decided to write a "how to" guide to fishing, it soon became clear as I attempted to organize the chapters that it would be unjust to present the varieties of ideas needed for successful angling into specific categories too exclusive from others. There would be a temptation for those who might be looking for shortcuts to skip the equipment chapter and go directly to the "where to find them" chapters. The results could be less than hoped for unless the entire picture is studied.

Therefore, I have deliberately intertwined what might be perceived by some as the most essential information with the main subject of each chapter, with the idea of helping the reader to more fully appreciate all of the aspects of crappie fishing. I really had little choice anyway, because the connections are crucial for successful fishing.

Imagine going into a great circular art museum with a domed top. In this museum there is only one very detailed painting; it covers the entire inside of the building. The only way one can fully appreciate the work of art is to walk up a spiral staircase. As the observer climbs he/she will inevitably catch glimpses of details to come while being reminded with each turn of the things already seen. But all this is necessary to see the true fullness of the painting. Crappie fishing is that painting. This book is intended to be the spiral staircase.

I have taken the liberty to write this manuscript in the first person with hopes that the reader will feel more at ease with this personal approach. In that same spirit most of the photos in the text were firsthand experiences. There are no "canned" or simulated shots. All the fish were caught and/or photographed in the wild; there are no aquarium fish displayed. And while it would have been easy enough to use underwater shots, I decided against it. After all, the angler has to locate crappies and their hiding places from above the surface. Where realistic photographs weren't possible or needed, simple line drawings were inserted. I felt that this was absolutely necessary to realistically maintain the integrity of the ideas.

INTRODUCTION

I wish to ask that wildlife officers from other states be forgiving that only Minnesota officers are shown in this first book. Because Minnesota officers are about to celebrate their first 100 years of service, I felt that I should honor them this way.

This book was not written to be an exhaustive collection of crappie fishing techniques. Instead, it's meant to present the most efficient methods overall. And because the most effective method involves the use of marabou jigs, I have devoted considerable space to explain the very satisfying craft of building your own lures.

To accommodate the reader I have included an appendix which contains certain better-known companies or suppliers which will be helpful for the angler's fishing needs. This was not done to recommend or endorse one over another but merely for convenience. Why confuse the reader by writing "The big catalog mail-order company out west" when the name would be more useful?

It has been a long journey from the first time I picked up a fishing pole to finally becoming an experienced angler. Most of the trophies I have collected along the way are memories: memories of trying to land my first redbreast bream from a shallow south Georgia ditch with a tin lima bean can at the age of six, or as a young soldier hooking my first Alaskan steelhead across the bay from Anchorage shortly after surviving the Good Friday earthquake. The humility learned from both trout and earthquake will never be forgotten.

Nor to be forgotten are all the folks along the way that have shared their fishing "secrets" with me. I still fondly recall my first childhood fishing lesson because of the number of times I had to be reminded, more than because of its importance. The lesson was based on the silly notion that you have to be real quiet when you fish or you will scare the fish off.

In later years as I learned better, I couldn't help but wonder if my mentors were either trying to hide from the game warden or simply trying to shut me up because I was driving them all crazy with too many fishing questions. All those annoying questions paid off. Now it's my turn to share by writing this first of what I hope to be a series of fishing books. I decided to start with crappies because of their wide geographic appeal among every age group.

There is a sense of spiritual renewal and aesthetic inspiration which sweeps over anglers when they are on the water. This has certainly been true for me. That inspiration became so intense that it drove me to become a conservationist at first by conviction and eventually by vocation as a wildlife officer. A certain unexplainable delight soothes my soul just to be able to physically communicate with the mysterious aquatic world of the fish through hook and line, or just to visit them in their world and learn as much about them as I can. I want others to experience those delights. And that is the purpose of this book.

SO THIS IS A CRAPPIE

From the great southern rivers and swamps to the deep crystal clear lakes of northern Minnesota and Wisconsin there is probably no freshwater fish that's more associated with spring angling than the crappie. Great numbers of expectant anglers line the shores while fishing boats crowd the surface of lakes and rivers during this period of the year. With the coming of spring, fishermen know that crappies will concentrate in the shallows and aggressively attack almost everything that's thrown at them. This usually occurs in late winter to early spring throughout the south and in late spring up north. And for a few weeks crappie fishing becomes a festival of entertainment for anglers of all ages. Then crappies seem to disappear.

Throughout the remainder of the year in each respective region these delectable creatures can be quite elusive and hard to find. Surely crappies must feed, whatever the season. So where do they go? Why should they be so hard to find? Except perhaps during the spring, anglers are starved for solid ideas on how and where to catch them. In the day to day contacts I make with fishermen the two most often asked questions are, "Where are the fish biting?" and "What are they catching them on?"

One amusing suggestion for finding good crappie fishing spots proposed by a sports writer illustrates very well the desperation among some for good ideas. He recommended that you should secretly follow elderly anglers as they leave bait shops and they will lead you right to their best fishing holes. Actually, your time could be better spent on the water looking for the fish yourself. Besides, you don't want to spend the better part of your day at the local police station trying to explain your behavior.

The fine art of catching fish successfully involves a lot more than just pointing people to a spot on the water or suggesting a lure or bait which they might not have with them anyway. Fortunately, in recent years there has been much written on angling techniques for walleyes, bass, northern pike, and other game fish. There remains a shortage of information available for crappie anglers, even though this fish is one of the most sought-after species.

So after many years of personal angling experience and research, and after observing, questioning, and comparing notes with thousands of anglers concerning their equipment, choice of baits, and lure selections, I shall attempt to present specific methods that will help crappie anglers fish successfully throughout the year. These methods are derived from an understanding of: 1) the crappies' habits; 2) their surroundings (habitat); 3) the use of the right equipment; 4) an appreciation for conservation principles.

To begin, let's look at the fish itself.

THERE ARE TWO TYPES OF CRAPPIES

Crappies are members of the sunfish family which includes large and smallmouth bass as well as the more commonly known bluegills, pumpkinseeds, and various other sunfish. Crappies can be subdivided into two separate species: the white crappie and the black crappie. Despite the dullness their names might suggest, these fish are dramatically colored and beautifully proportioned.

Both species are widely distributed throughout most of the United States, and it's not uncommon to find both in the same rivers and lakes in many parts of the country. Black crappies can be found from Florida to the southernmost part of some provinces of Canada. They find the clear, cooler lakes of the north more to their liking than does the white crappie. White crappies are not as common in the far north since they are more at home in warmer, turbid rivers, lakes, and reservoirs.

Usually with a glance you can determine whether a crappie is black or white by the distinct markings on its sides. But occasionally you will catch some that will be missing all of their coloration because of their prolonged lack of contact with light; the crappie will then have a silvery appearance with no markings.

While fishing for crappies in a Texas reservoir I caught a few absolutely colorless fish from beneath a canopy of logs known locally as the Belton Reservoir Log Jam. The log jam seemed to cover acres

SO THIS IS A CRAPPIE

The white crappie is usually found in warm and slightly turbid waters. Note the brightly colored lure used for its visibility in such waters.

Black Crappie

of water and provided an excellent sun shade for light shy fish. Hiding beneath the log jam the crappies had seen little light and appeared almost to be made of glass. They were missing all of their distinguishing color markings. Even so, they were easily identifiable by other physical clues.

TELLING THEM APART

WHITE CRAPPIES

1) In most situations the most obvious way to identify a white crappie is the presence of five to ten dark vertical blotches or stripes running from top to bottom on the side of the fish.

2) In the absence of markings, whites are most easily distinguishable by the presence of four to seven (but most often six) stiff sharp spinal rays located at the front of their dorsal fins. The dorsal fin is located on the crappie's back.

3) If you look closely you can see that the white crappie has a greater distance from its eye to the front of its dorsal fin than the distance along the base of that dorsal fin. On the black crappie the dorsal fin base length and the distance from the front of that fin to the eye is the same.

4) Whites have more of a tapered back toward the head, making them appear more slender than the blacks.

5) The eyes of a white crappie are usually yellow to yellow/green.

6) The white crappie is pale in color compared to the black, and it generally looks whiter, hence its name. (see photo). It has silvery sides washed with a hint of light olive green or pale yellow except for the dark vertical bands mentioned above. Its dorsal, caudal, and anal fins are beautifully arrayed with alternate dark and light spots. The top of its back is colored in dark olive green with many hues of blue, green, and silvery reflections.

BLACK CRAPPIES

1) The stiff dorsal spines of the black crappie will vary from six to nine, but almost always number seven or eight.

2) The sides of the blacks will be mottled with black blotches or spots. They will not have the vertical bands found on the whites.

3) The black crappie's back forms a higher arch than does that of the white.

4) The length of the base of the dorsal fin equals the distance from the eye to the front of that fin.

5) Black crappies' eyes are yellow or sometimes yellow/brown.

6) I believe that there is no freshwater fish that can compare in beauty to the black crappie especially during spawning season. The calico pattern of black spots on a background of silver and gold led one small child to call them angel fish. He explained that anything so beautiful must be from heaven. The huge graceful speckled fins and tail do suggest a resemblance to butterfly wings. The black's back is colored with either black or dark olive green, and as you turn this "angel" in the sunlight you can see various shades of blue washed into the top half of the back and around the face.

When both species inhabit the same waters they will occasionally hybridize, making identification so difficult that sometimes only a fisheries specialist can identify them properly.

THE BEST CRAPPIE BAIT

Neither the black or white crappie would be seen as angels by their fellow water creatures. They have a voracious, merciless appetite and will eat small crustaceans, aquatic insects, minnows, other small species of fish, and even each other if the other is small enough. Because very small minnows are a favorite crappie meal, anglers who use minnows or minnow imitating lures are the most successful at catching white and black crappies.

In most situations minnow imitating lures will even out-produce live bait.

The only time lures will not be more effective than live bait is when the water temperatures are below 50 degrees or at night. There are a variety of lures which crappies will hit, including small lead head jigs, spinners, streamers, and artificial flies. Occasionally crappies will perplex the experienced angler by mysteriously attacking the most unexpected targets.

One winter afternoon I was drift fishing on the spectacularly beautiful Shingle Creek near Kissimee, Florida. In Florida, crappies are known as speckled perch. As unbelievable as it may seem, I observed a very old angler catch a crappie on a bare hook. No, I hadn't followed him. But here was someone with a secret I had to learn! It turned out that he, too, was amazed at this feat.

His unbaited hook had fallen back into the water while he was placing a fish he had just caught onto his stringer. Apparently as the dropped hook slowly fluttered downward it attracted a crappie. The angler's rod began to throb against the side of the boat. The astonished old gentleman grabbed his pole and landed a 1½ pound black crappie! As minnows swim about and change direction their shiny undersides will flash in the water and reflect light much like the flash codes made by a kid playing with a mirror in the sun. The descending tiny gold hook must have appeared to be a minnow to the mixed up crappie as it flashed and fluttered downward.

As unusual as it is for a crappie to eat a barely visible unbaited hook, consider an incident that happened while I was angling with a buddy in a city lake in Minnesota. My friend was casting a very large floating musky lure into shallow water hoping to attract a large pike. Just as he was about to lift it from the water to recast, a male crappie no larger than the lure in full spawning color slammed into the musky plug impaling itself on the hooks. Since he could not have been trying to eat something as big as himself, the only reasonable explanation was that he was aggressively trying to defend his nest from what he perceived to be a threat.

Crappies attacking bare hooks and musky lures (however delightful the idea) are, of course, rare and extreme examples. This noble fish is

SO THIS IS A CRAPPIE

much more predictable than that. These types of behavior simply illustrates humbling exceptions to this all important rule for crappie fishing:

Smaller lures or minnows are the key to successful crappie fishing. Of all possible lure selections, nothing is more effective than small lead head jigs.

THE LEAD HEAD JIG

The effectiveness of the small lead head jig was demonstrated by one of the state of Minnesota's most publicized, although not the largest, crappie over the limit cases. A man and three others were found in possession of 754 crappies. The illustrated newspaper account erred because the four individuals were entitled under Minnesota law to possess only 15 crappies apiece. Altogether the number of fish in possession should not have been over 60. The men were 694 crappies over the limit! What was the secret of their success (until they were discovered)? They were using a $1/32$ ounce lead head jig.

THE CRAPPIES EYES:
THE KEY TO SUCCESSFUL ANGLING

Crappies are primarily sight feeders. As you study the physical make up of these fish you will notice that the eyes of crappies are located quite high on their heads. Their field of view is basically forward and upward, virtually ignoring everything outside of this zone. Because of the location of their eyes they prey upon smaller creatures unfortunate enough to swim slowly overhead. If you place a small lure in their sight zone you'd better have a grip on your fishing rod.

I have tested this numerous times by jigging scented lures as well as minnows erratically behind and below crappies with no results. I would then place the same lure or bait in front of the fish in a slightly elevated position and experience an immediate attack. Unscented lures tested in the same way had exactly the same effect. When I would place a lure lower than their eye level it would not be attacked since the fish could not see it.

I've used this technique when fishing crappies in clear water around flooded timber to prevent smaller crappies from taking my lures. When I would see a smaller fish approach my lure as I was slowly lowering it through the tree branches, I would wait until just before the fish hit, then drop it deeper. The confused crappie would lose sight of the jig and frantically swim about looking up for it. Even in turbid waters crappies still rely almost entirely on their vision to feed. Since they cannot see as far under such conditions it becomes necessary to move your bait or lure slower and closer to their cover.

SO THIS IS A CRAPPIE!

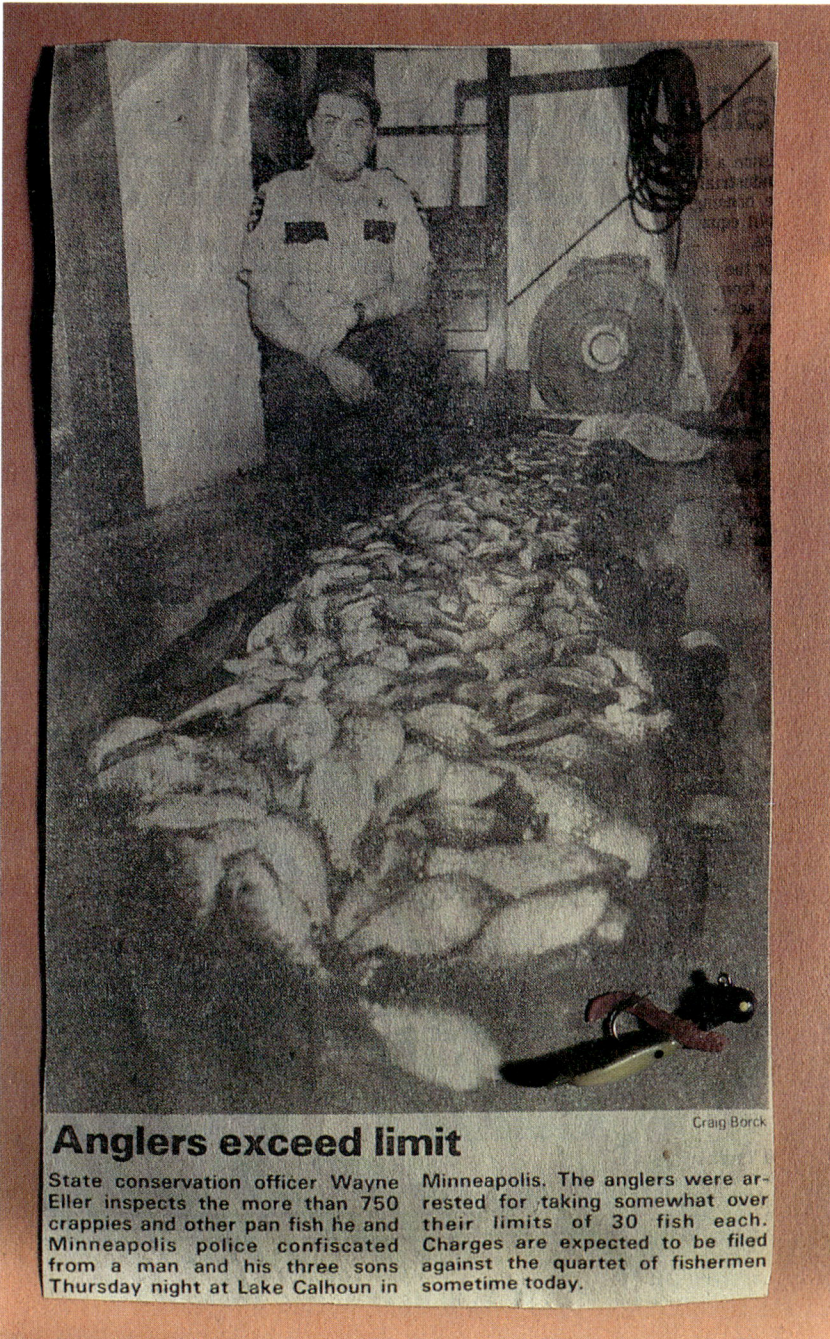

A page from the author's scrapbook. A lead head jig was used to catch the crappies featured in this St. Paul Dispatch and Pioneer Press *newspaper story (reprinted with permission).*

SO THIS IS A CRAPPIE!

Since a crappie's eyes are located almost in a fixed stare skyward, one would think that it would be fairly accustomed to light. This is not the case. Crappies appear to be the most light sensitive of the sunfishes with a definite preference for low light or even dark situations.

An understanding of this low light preference plays an enormous role in angling success because crappies will seek the shadows of objects or depth to escape the blinding rays of the sun. We will return to this subject later.

SMELL

A crappie's sense of smell plays a minimum role in overall angling success. Even at night a crappie will rely on his vision or his ability to detect the slightest movement with his lateral line to feed. The lateral line is a highly sophisticated pressure sensitive organ which runs along each side of a fish. The lateral line can be clearly seen as a thin dark line that runs nearly the full length of the fish. It is so sensitive that totally blind fish can still survive by reading their environment and ambushing prey using this pressure and vibration sensitive organ. Certainly crappies take some bait because of its smell, but they will take it sooner if they first see or detect it with their lateral line.

A crappie does have a keen sense of smell, but its significance to the angler except for negative odors is unimportant compared to sight, and to an extent, vibration. Under no circumstances should you fish with a lure or line that has been contaminated with gasoline, mosquito spray, suntan lotion, or any other unnatural odor. You will increase your catch by carefully washing your hands to remove perspiration before tying on a lure or adding new line to your reel or pole.

Crappies can be smelly little things themselves. During the spawning season the scales and skin of the male crappie takes on a distinctively strong odor. The male crappies are the ones which establish and guard nesting sites. Perhaps their odor serves to warn off other males from the nest or to attract females to it; maybe both. However, once the skin is off and he's in the frying pan you won't notice it. The spawning female also has a slight odor, but it's not as noticeable.

WATER TEMPERATURES

Crappies are extremely sensitive to temperature differences. And this sensitivity plays a major role in their behavior. Most important, it determines the season for spawning activity. Responding to the change in the water's temperature, crappies will begin to establish their nest on spawning surfaces or platforms when the water immediately around that site approaches 67 degrees F.

White crappies will generally spawn between 61 F. to 68 F. Blacks will spawn between 64 F. and 68 F., but have been observed doing so at colder temperatures. Although it is not a hard and fast rule, 67 degrees is a good indicator for peak spawning activity. Spawning surfaces are usually hard-packed, heat absorbent sand, clay, gravel, aquatic plant roots, fallen tree trunks, or occasionally mud. Black crappies show a preference for spawning near live aquatic vegetation.

Temperature also affects a crappie's location at times other than during spawning season because the fish seeks the most comfortable water to avoid excessive heat or cold. When water stratifies during midsummer and again in winter, crappies can be found heavily schooled together all at the same depth as they seek preferred temperature ranges.

CRAPPIE SIZE

The average crappie on a stringer or in the live well will range between 1/4 pound to 1 1/2 pounds depending on the body of water being fished. They will vary in average size from lake to lake. Because of their ecological systems, some lakes always seem to produce large fish. Others will seem to have an abundance of smaller, stunted fish.

I have heard and read countless ideas on how to predict which ecological system should consistently produce larger fish. The most practical way to make that determination is to check with bait shops in the area where you wish to fish or to watch for fishing contest results which are faithfully published by some newspapers.

If an angler is interested in catching trophy-sized crappies he/she should fish only those lakes in his region that have a continuous history of huge fish. Try to avoid lakes which only occasionally will produce "slabs" (as the big ones are called). It has been my observation that the biggest crappies over all come from large rivers or lakes which are connected to large rivers.

WORLD RECORD CRAPPIES

Most anglers have their own ideas of what is a good sized fish. A favorite crappie-fishing uncle, who can spin fish stories with the best of them, lives near the Santee-Cooper Reservoir in my home state of South Carolina. He tells how he prefers to keep 'em only if they're big enough to fit on his boat paddle handle, which he claims he uses for a fish stringer. Even though the world record black crappie does come from the Santee-Cooper, weighing in at a monstrous five pounds, dear Uncle's boat paddle story might be stretching it a little. There are some mammouth-sized crappies caught there, though, and two to three pounders are not at all uncommon. The world's record white crappie came from the Enid Reservoir in Mississippi and weighed 5 pounds and 3 ounces.

Certainly, the southern states can be proud of these huge fish, but they grow them big up north too. Minnesota, in fact, ties the world record black crappie with a 5 pounder of its own, taken from the Vermillion River near the town of Hastings. Of course, such huge fish are uncommon and many anglers are perfectly content to go home with a nice "mess" of 1/4 pounders. A couple anglers I met on the

Trout River near Saint Augustine, Florida, figured that if a crappie "fits between two pieces of bread, it's a keeper."

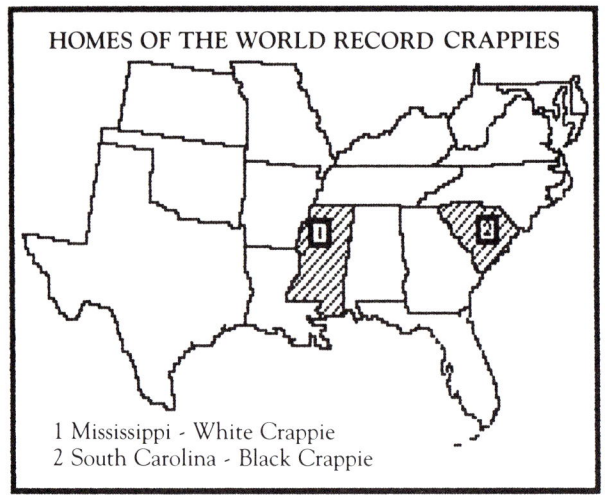

DETERMINING A CRAPPIE'S WEIGHT FROM ITS LENGTH

Crappies weights can be fairly accurately estimated by their length. The following chart was compiled by John Dobie in the, **Fisheries Manager's Handbook; Minnesota Department of Conservation Special Publication #82; 1970.**

INCHES	7	8	9	10	11	12	13	14	15	16	17
LBS.		.3	.4	.5	.7	.8	1	1.3	1.5	1.5	2.4	2.9

THE BEST TIME FOR FISHING UNDER ALL CONDITIONS

MOON PHASES

The old adage that the best time for fishing is whenever you get a chance may be cute and clever, but it really doesn't help the serious crappie angler. Nor do the myths built around *solunar tables* which supposedly help predict the peak hours for fishing by the phases and locations of the sun and moon. Interestingly, the belief that observations of the moon's phases will reveal the best fishing opportunities is very prevalent in the southern coastal states. I suppose it is because the effect of the moon on tides and salt water life is rather apparent there. So it's not unreasonable for some of the folks there to believe that the moon would also influence freshwater fish. However, for purposes of crappie angling this is simply not true. Furthermore, there is no scientific evidence which supports such a claim.

BAROMETRIC PRESSURE

Worrying about barometric pressure changes negatively affecting crappie fishing is popular in the midwest and northern states. Crappie fisherman should totally disregard barometric pressure changes and wind direction predictions (unless they're interested in the weather for boating safety reasons). One of the greatest myths perpetrated about why fish bite or refuse to bite is the idea that barometric pressure changes will directly affect their appetites.

I've checked many anglers who use pressure changes as an explanation for being fishless, yet, I have never seen a barometer in a boat. So, of course, there would have been no way for them to determine what the barometer was doing at the time. On the same body of water another fishing party would have several nice fish, which would certainly cast doubt on the first boat's reasoning. Barometric changes make little difference to a hungry crappie.

While these myths add interest and color to fishing conversations, they have little or no effect on crappie fishing and are about as helpful as sticking voodoo pins in a crappie doll. Yes, to some degree these factors can have some effect on some creatures, but the crappie angler should completely ignore them.

COLD FRONTS

Even the beginning angler soon learns that crystal clear skies accompanied by a drop in temperatures can signal poor fishing. For reasons never fully explained to my satisfaction, but nonetheless true, fish are simply not very active during the day with the passing of a cold front through an area. Even professional fisheries' managers will cease net sampling operations during intense cold front movements.

Cold fronts usually bring clear blue cloudless skies; there is virtually no moisture content in the air. While cold fronts are usually accompanied by higher barometer readings, it's not the pressure that makes the difference to fish. Rather it's the lack of moisture in the air. Such moisture either in the form of high humidity or clouds normally serves as a filter to block short, ultraviolet solar radiation. With a passing of a cold front the filter disappears, allowing an increased penetration of this type of radiation which can be hazardous to fish. This seems to be the most likely cause for decreased fish activity during weather conditions brought in by a cold front.

You and I can protect ourselves to some degree with sunglasses, suntan lotions, and clothing. A crappie must escape to very deep water or hide in thick vegetation, not really caring to move about much. This does not mean that fish can't be caught during cold fronts. In fact, rivers are only mildly affected by cold fronts. If you have a river in your area, you'll be better off fishing there until the skies begin to cloud again. If you must fish in a lake, you'll just have to work a little harder.

DAWN AND DUSK: THE BEST TIME TO FISH

There are always some fish on any given day in any body of water that are hungry and will bite. But crappies bite best and can be caught in greater numbers within a two-hour period on each side of sunrise and sunset, without regard to barometric pressure changes, wind direction, moon phases, or even cold fronts.

Most important, whenever you decide to fish, if you follow the fishing recommendations in the following chapters precisely, your success at fishing crappies will be inevitable. The shared ideas that follow were derived from nearly a million casts, several thousand crappies caught (and released), and years of observing anglers both as a hobby and a profession.

The Secret of the Marabou Jig
The Ultimate Crappie Lure

THE ULTIMATE CRAPPIE LURE

There is nothing more devastating to a fish population than a determined angler armed with an assortment of small minnow-imitating lead head jigs.

A lead head jig is a special shaped hook which has been placed into a mold where molten lead is poured to form a small head near the eye of the hook.

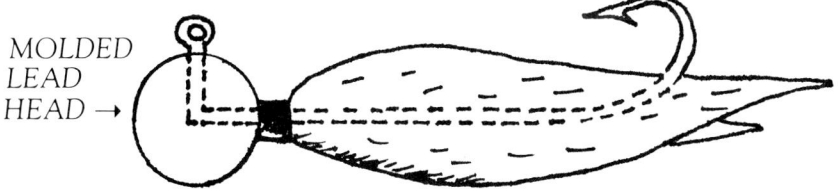

MOLDED LEAD HEAD →

DRESSING OF FEATHERS
OR OTHER MATERIALS

The hook is then embellished with colorful feathers, plastic, animal fur, synthetic fiber, chenille, or even tinsel; the lead head is usually painted. There are several excellent color combinations and hook dressings which will attract fish. These inexpensive little fish catchers can be purchased at any bait and tackle shop.

Not only do lead head jigs come in a variety of colors and materials, but they can be found in a variety of sizes. Jig sizes are measured by the weight of their lead heads. Generally, they are available in the following sizes: 1/64 oz.; 1/32 oz.; 1/16 oz.; 1/8 oz.; 1/4 oz.; and 1/2 oz.

The jig size that will catch more crappies is the 1/32 ounce.

THE BEST COMBINATION

There are four main considerations for selecting the most effective crappie jig: size (weight); color; hook dressing; length (something that few anglers think about).

Of all the possible effective combinations of color, size, and hook decorations, there is one jig that clearly may be the most outstanding crappie-catching lure ever tied on the end of a line. I have introduced a lot of crappies to the frying pan with this magnificently effective lure.

A crappie lure with a seemingly magical quality is a 1/32 oz. jig with a pink head and a yellow marabou (stork) feathered body tied with a collar of red nylon thread.

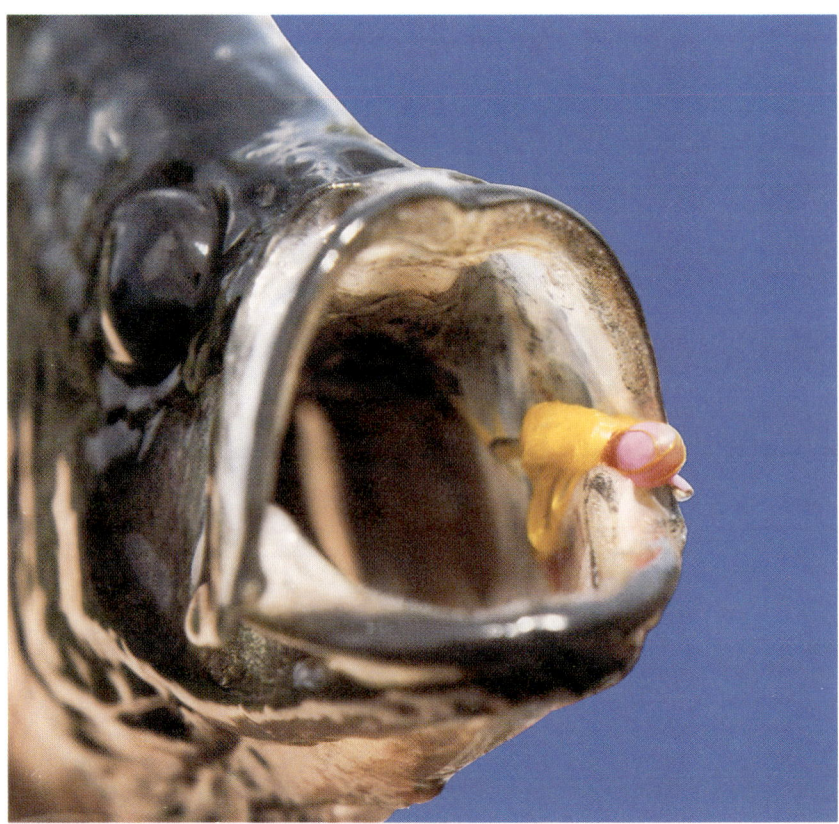

The ultimate crappie lure: a pink and yellow jig.

COLOR

PINK/YELLOW

Crappie lures with the combined colors of pink and yellow are the most effective. Pink/yellow is overall more effective simply because of its visibility. Remember, crappies are sight feeders. Most bodies of water will have some tint of coloration. Some are tannin stained and look like tea, others are greenish from algal growth, and still others may be silty gray. Even in crystal clear lakes there is usually some type of background coloration because of vegetation, dead trees, stones and sand bars. No matter what the coloration of the water tint or background, the visibility of a pink/yellow lure is sufficient in almost every situation to provide enough contrast to be seen by crappies.

Remember the angler who was discovered in possession of 754 crappies? Please look back at his lure which is superimposed on the newspaper clipping illustrated on page 7. It was a 1/32 oz. jig. Interestingly, while the dressing he used was not feathers, he had attached two plastic tails on a hook to get the combined color effect of pink and yellow and made news with it.

BLACK

There is one other color which rivals the pink/yellow; Black! Black is extremely effective during spawning time for catching both male and female crappies.

The explanation for the effectiveness of the color black is much more involved than that of the pink/yellow. Male crappies of both the white and black species, begin to turn velvet black during spawning season. This coloration change is more pronounced in the black species but is equally unmistakable in the white. The males of both species have the responsibility to locate, maintain, and safeguard spawning sites. The black coloration peaks when the males have established their nests. This color change seems to have three main purposes.

First, this is a male's signal to a female crappie that he has established a nest; it's his invitation for her to deposit her eggs at that site. Secondly, it's a warning to other males to stay away from his real estate. Finally, the dark color may be a form of camouflage which allows crappies to spawn on shallow dead trees with less fear of attack from birds of prey.

The color black used as a signal to other crappies is known as a *Super-Normal Stimulus*. This color change becomes the main controlling stimulation which attracts females and repels other males. It triggers aggressive behavior among both males and females, behavior that is not characteristic of them throughout the rest of the year. Females will instinctively swim toward the color stimulus knowing a nesting site has been prepared at that location. Males will charge at black objects placed near their nest, actually ramming them at times.

Color change and spawning readiness is brought on primarily by rising water temperatures and perhaps the angle of the sun. Crappies will spawn when water reaches approximately 67° F. Temperatures will not be the same everywhere in a body of water. Different locations in a lake can vary as much as 15 to 20 degrees. Because of the various locations of crappies throughout the different temperature ranges, some of them will be ready to spawn a few days prior to others. In fact, spawning readiness can even vary among individual fish in a given community.

Because of differences between individual fish, some females may begin to bunch up (aggregate)* near spawning areas a few days before the males are ready for them. They begin to search aggressively for the males with the new black velvet coats and are attracted to any object of that color.

During spawning season both male and female crappies will viciously attack black lures.

If you cast a black lure into this aggregate of females, the super-normal stimulation caused by that color will trigger an immediate response; you will definitely have their attention. But, of course, one crappie pretty much knows what another crappie looks like. So, the initial mating response will be gone as soon as the female swims close enough to realize it's not a potential mate. However, since she is already in an aggressive mood, and after all, since the object of her attention is small enough to swallow, she figures what the heck, and eats it!

FOOTNOTE:
*Crappies don't actually school, they aggregate.

Once crappies are actually on their nests they become aggressive toward almost any trespasser which they think might threaten the deposited eggs or the newly hatched fry (baby fish). At this point the color is not that important for catching females, although a pink/yellow jig is usually the most easily seen. The male will attack most colors and for that matter almost anything near their beds once they have their own nesting site established. However, black is still considered a great threat by males because it appears at first to be another male looking for a spawning site of his own.

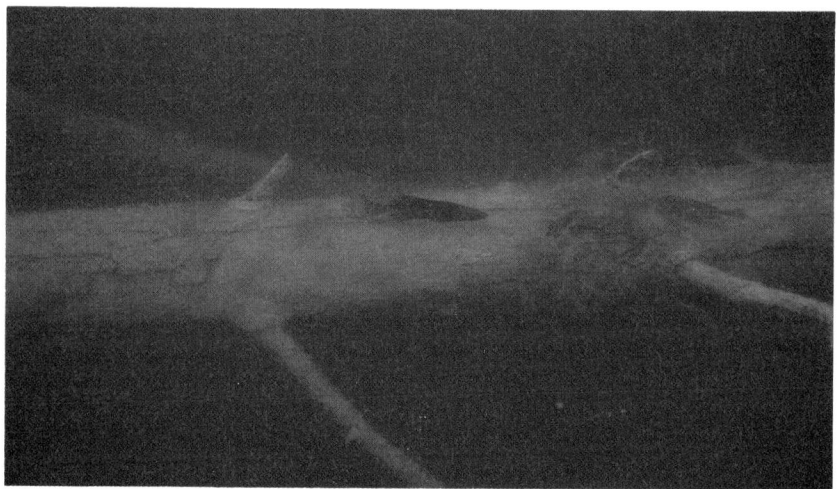

Above: A male crappie keeps vigil over eggs trying to prevent the pesky bluegills from robbing his nest. Below: The crappie charges the sunfish who pushed their luck by moving in too close. A lure placed too close to the nest will receive the same treatment.

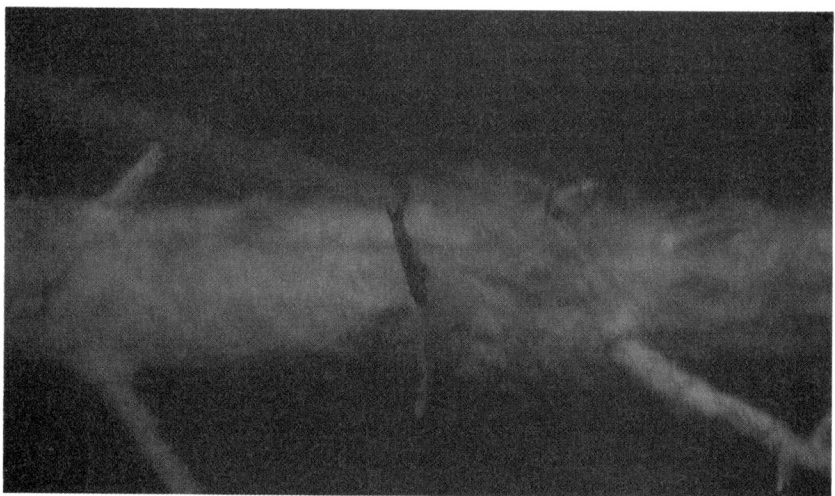

BLACK IS VICIOUSLY ATTACKED BY NESTING MALES.

Countless times I've slowly drifted my boat over communities of spawning beds to study them. My boat is equipped with an electric trolling motor which happens to be black. I prefer to leave the electric motor off when drifting over nests, as it can create a vortex, a miniature underwater tornado, which I fear might disturb the eggs or harm the fry. On numerous occasions as the silent, nearly motionless black motor would drift through the immediate area of a nest it would be attacked by protective jealous males.

A nice stringer of spawning crappies for these two youngsters. Both were using black marabou jigs.

Super-normal stimuli and nest protection reaction are not the only reasons crappies attack during spawn; They're just plain hungry, too. A male crappie guarding his nest day after day has no opportunity to hunt and will readily vacuum in small lures placed in front and slightly above him.

While crappies are on their beds they are very vulnerable. An angler who finds them can pick every one of them off their nests. Crappies seem quite capable of reproducing rapidly in most areas and would not be threatened by heavy harvesting. A female crappie will produce from 30,000 to 188,000 eggs, depending on her age and health. Yet only a small percentage of these eggs will eventually mature to angling-size fish.

On any given lake there will be numerous isolated spawning areas. But every lake is different and some are just not capable consistently of yielding good populations of fish without special measures. Some states have set aside spawning areas where crappies may not be fished while they are on their beds; the future of good fishing depends on compliance with conservation ethics and regulations.

This two pound female lying across the five gallon pail above was capable of depositing close to a hundred thousand eggs in the nest of a male crappie.

Note the milt extracted from the male crappie which fertilizes the eggs.

LENGTH OF THE LURE

There is a specific length, which when combined with the colors above, should guarantee even the novice angler fish in his creel: Exactly one and one-half inches long.

Black or pink/yellow jigs are so effective on crappies that they approach being unfair. Yet, almost unbelievably even this effectiveness can be improved upon. One hot summer day while fishing on the beautiful St. Croix river on the boundary between Wisconsin and Minnesota, I made one of the most significant discoveries of my crappie angling experience. I was casting a small 1/32 ounce yellow-bodied marabou jig into an eddy which pooled up alongside some fierce river white water. I had caught several nice crappies (both black and white) which were resting in the quiet water just out of reach of the rush and roar of the main flow of the river.

I noticed that I'd had several bites which resulted in nothing but disappointment when I set the hook. I thought that possibly the tail of the jig might be too long. Perhaps the crappies were only grabbing the tip of the lure's tail. I decided to shorten the feathers. I pinched off about an eighth of an inch and discovered that I was no longer losing as many fish.

I decided to take off more of the tail. Again there was an improvement. Once again I shortened the jig. At this point I caught a fish on every cast! As any crappie angler soon finds out, you won't land every fish. Some will simply pull free. Even after this last length adjustment a fish would occasionally pull off. But before I could complete the retrieve to cast again, another crappie had grabbed the lure. Amazingly, I caught and released 150 crappies in one hour with the last adjustment!

To further test this discovery I began to alternate the lure. Several times I switched the shortened one with other jigs with longer tails. The results were the same as before. I would catch some fish with the longer ones, but I would get several strikes without hooking the attacker. The crappies were coming up from behind and underneath to grab the jig but were only getting a mouthful of feathers. I would retie the shortened lure and WHAM! A fish on every cast! I was so afraid that I'd lose this lure that I stopped fishing with it, went home, and measured its length. *IT WAS EXACTLY ONE AND ONE-HALF INCHES LONG!*

In my excitement I had forgotten to try lures which were shorter than this. However, on subsequent trips I've also tested shorter ones with only fair results. I found that the shorter lures did not generate the same number of bites as the one and one-half inch lure.

WEIGHT

A crappie angler has only a few weight classes of lures which will work well for him; they range from the 1/62 ounce through the 1/16 oz. But, just as there is one color combination and one exact length that is more effective, this is also true for the most effective size (weight). And this size is the 1/32 ounce. There are two reasons why the 1/32 oz. jig is the best weight.

First and most significant, this 1/32 ounce weight sinks in the water at a very slow rate allowing crappies a chance to look it over before it sinks out of sight. A heavier lure would drop too fast. Crappies do not have the speed of most freshwater predators and prefer slow-moving targets.

The slower you can move a lure in the water the more crappies you will catch.

Secondly, the 1/32 oz. jig can be easily cast with spinning gear without adding cumbersome weights or bobbers which often distracts fish or causes the angler to lose control and sensitivity. If the jig is lighter it can't be cast properly, and if it's any heavier, it sinks too fast for crappies. *In most situations it must be 1/32 ounce.*

HOOK DRESSING

Jig hooks can be dressed with a variety of materials. *The two materials I recommend above all others are soft plastics and marabou (stork) feathers*. The soft plastic-bodied jigs are molded to look like minnows or formed with the now familiar curled tails which wiggle when retrieved through the water. Marabou feathers, when used, are tied to the collar of the jigs and are formed to imitate minnows and small aquatic insects.

One of the most positive things about the plastic jigs is cost. Relative to most jigs, these little crappie catchers are priced within the budgets of most anglers, whereas many of the more exotic ones can be expensive. As you will see later, to catch crappies, you are going to have to fish in some places where you will lose lures; therefore, cost is important.

Plastic jigs do have their drawbacks. After the first five or six fish the plastic bodies tear away from the hook and their effectiveness is destroyed. Worse yet, those with curly tails will constantly hang up on timber and reeds. They'll nearly drive you mad constantly trying to free up your lures which seem to wrap their twisting little tails around everything they come into contact with. And usually when you've freed them, their tails are gone or just about ripped away. Nonetheless, their effectiveness is second only to marabou and are highly recommended.

From my experience, marabou feathers are unsurpassed in fish-attracting reliability. Nothing! Nothing! Nothing will outproduce marabou feathers as a dressing for lures to fish for crappies. Certainly there are more durable materials, but they simply do not catch crappies as well.

Why is the marabou better? First, the soft flexible feathers actually seem to pulsate in water with the slightest movement giving the appearance of being some sort of living thing. This cannot be said of any other material.

Next, because of the near-waterproof quality of marabou, it will hold its form or body for hours without shrinking down. After being in water for only a short time other types of feathers lose their shape and look almost like a single strand of hair.

A fish which attacks a marabou jig is getting little else but hook in its mouth. There is little bulk or mass in a marabou body because it's made of puffy feathers. Certainly, hook-setting ability is improved if the fish is biting down on sharp pointed steel of the hook instead of plastic, hair, tinsel, or chenille.

The fourth positive thing about marabou as a dressing is its durability. The strength of marabou is quite surprising for a feather. Although the fish will unknowingly be grabbing the hook much of the time, especially if the lure is the right length, they will occasionally grab only the feathers. But with marabou feathers there will be virtually no damage to the body.

Of course, the individual barbs of feather easily break. But since several barbs are placed together to form the body of the lure, durability is given to the construction. The hundreds of small cross veins of barbules found in the vane of the feather interlock with one another to form a braided rope-like strength to prevent tearing.

Additionally, the interlocking glossy feather barbules reflect light in the water, which realistically imitate the flashes of minnows turning on their side, as they dart about.

Finally, on those occasions where the crappie doesn't bite the hook, the chance is quite good that their raspy little teeth or their gills will become entangled on the marabou, giving the angler an additional split second to set the hook. The thousands of radiated barbules on each barb has much the same effect on a crappie's mouth as two pieces of material joined by velcro. This occurs because of the design of a crappie's gills and the presence of hundreds of nearly microscopic teeth arranged along the lips (mandibles) of the fish. Marabou easily clings to teeth and gills.

Although the primary function of a crappie's gills is to enable it to glean dissolved oxygen from the water, its gills appear to be further specialized for catching and holding prey. Based on careful observations I've made on the high numbers of gill-hooked crappies, I believe that a crappie uses its gills as well its teeth to help capture prey as it sifts food from the water. When a crappie flares his gills to vacuum in water and food, his gills allow water to move easily through but will not allow aquatic insects or minnows to escape. When a marabou jig is netted by the fish's gills, the thousands of barbules entangle themselves on the gills. The fish can't as easily spit the lure out.

There are two major problems with using marabou lures. First, the lifelike, pulsating marabou tied on a $1/32$ ounce lead-head jig in black or pink/yellow is so convincing that many other species of freshwater fish are caught on it. It can be quite a nuisance (but I bet you won't mind) while trying to have a nice relaxing day fishing crappies, to have to constantly fight off bass, pike, walleyes, and other fish which can't resist this lure.

The numerous small crappie teeth (top) cling easily to the hundreds of criss-cross barbules of the marabou feather (bottom).

While fishing crappies with a fellow conservation officer in central Minnesota, we caught and released over 50 northern pike in just a few hours using these jigs. In fact, we caught walleyes, sunfish, and even a dogfish. Oh yes! We also got our crappies.

The most amazing thing that I've caught to date on one of these fantastic lures was a loon! Thank goodness I was able to get the loon off with little more than its dignity hurt.

OTHER FISH

Although the 1/32 oz. pink/yellow jig is the best overall crappie lure, it should be modified when other fish are targeted. The following chart will be helpful for determining the best weight, color, and length of marabou lures for catching many common game fish.

FISH	WEIGHT	HEAD COLOR	DRESSING COLOR	LENGTH
BASS (LM)	1/4 oz.	Black	Black	2 3/4 in.
	1/4 oz.	Pink	Yellow	2 3/4 in.
BASS (SM)	1/32 oz.	Black	Black	1 1/2 in.
	1/8 oz.	Pink	Yellow	2 in.
BLUEGILLS	1/64 oz.	Pink	Black	3/4 in.
	1/64 oz.	Pink	Yellow	3/4 in.
NORTHERNS	1/4 oz.	Pink	Yellow	2 3/4 in.
	1/4 oz.	Orange	Orange/White	2 3/4 in.
RAINBOWS	1/64 oz.	Orange	Orange/White	3/4 in.
	1/32 oz.	Orange	Black	1 3/4 in.
WALLEYES	1/4 oz.	Orange	White	2 3/4 in.
	1/4 oz.	Orange	Orange/White	2 3/4 in.
WHITE BASS	1/16 oz.	White	White	1 1/2 in.
	1/32 oz.	Yellow	Yellow	1 1/2 in.

Yes, fishing with this marvelous lure has its drawbacks, but catching all those extra species of fish is the price you have to pay for success.

The second problem with using marabou jigs is a bit more serious. It is very difficult to find a supplier for affordable quality marabou jigs without having to pawn your boat. They can be quite expensive compared to the plastic jigs, but they are much more effective.

You can save a lot of money by making your own lures. The following chapter will include illustrations and instructions on how to make marabou jigs. You can buy the materials at almost any well-stocked tackle and sports shop. If you wish to fish with the pink/yellow 1/32 ounce one and a half-inch marabou jig, you will definitely have to make your own, as I am not aware of any such combination being currently marketed. By making your own jigs you will be able to combine all the key ingredients of size length, color, and dressing for maximum fishing success.

Although this northern pike was glutted with the partially digested sunfish shown here being removed, the pike, nonetheless, could not resist the pink/ yellow marabou jig.

MAKING AND USING THE MARABOU JIG

I have spent many enjoyable relaxing hours tying my own lures. The time spent at this hobby has been very rewarding, providing me with successful fishing and with quiet times to reflect on the blessings of our natural resources. I have grown to look forward with reverence to my lure tying as a time of relaxation and contemplation.

Oh well! Contemplation doesn't catch fish; marabou jigs do. And, they're quite easy to make. In just a few easy steps you can tie your own lures with little effort. You will spend about $ .08 to $ .20 for each lure instead of $ .60 to $ 1.00 for manufactured ones. Your costs will vary depending on the supplier and the volume of your purchase.

You can buy the materials at almost any well-stocked tackle and sports shop. Additionally, many mail order fishing tackle supply companies have these materials. For the convenience of the reader I have noted a couple mail order companies in appendix A.

The main components you will need to purchase are:

1) **UNPAINTED $1/32$ OUNCE PRE-MOLDED LEAD JIG HEADS ON NUMBER SIX HOOKS.** If at all possible get those with bendable gold-colored hooks.

The lead head must have a collar extending back along the shaft of the hook, ending with a small bead. The bead prevents the tied feathers from slipping off.

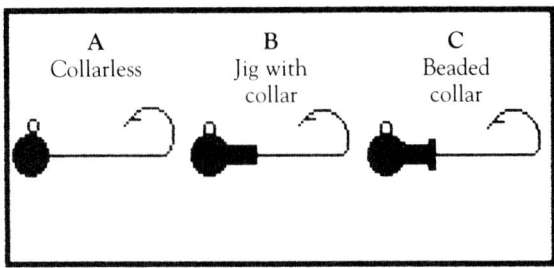

Never use collarless jigs (A). Try to avoid beadless collars (B). Only use beaded collars (C). If you are unable to find beaded collars, you can take wire cutters or some other tool to make a dent in the beadless collar's soft lead which will prevent the thread and feathers from slipping off the collar.

Stiff hooks are considerably more difficult to dislodge from the crappie's mouth or to free up when caught on rocks, timber, or reeds. The gold color adds a little additional flash. Some anglers believe that it is important to hide their hooks. This is a myth that must be ignored. Remember the old angler who caught the crappie on a bare hook (Chap. 1).

2) **MARABOU FEATHERS IN COLORS OF BLACK AND YELLOW.** To get the pink/yellow combination it's best to paint the head of the lure pink with a yellow, feathered body. To add interest to your collection of jigs you might consider other colors as well. My third choice following pink/yellow and black is white.

In crystal clear lakes with little vegetation, white can be a devastating crappie killer when a small amount of pink is added.

3) **RED NYLON THREAD IN NUMBER ⅔ SIZE** (It is sometimes called size number 00.) Red thread is used to tie the marabou to the collars of the jigs. Red is preferable because it presents an impressionistic resemblance to the gills of a minnow. Nylon is both strong and water resistant.

4) **A THREAD BOBBIN TO DISPENSE THREAD WHILE TYING MARABOU TO THE JIG COLLAR.** I cannot recommend the purchase of commercially produced bobbins. They are too expensive for heavy use because they wear out much too quickly. Constant use will wear grooves into the tip end of the bobbin, which will cut your thread prematurely.

You can make an excellent bobbin from an old clothes hanger or an empty 35mm plastic film canister. As soon as you see wear starting to appear, throw it away and make another.

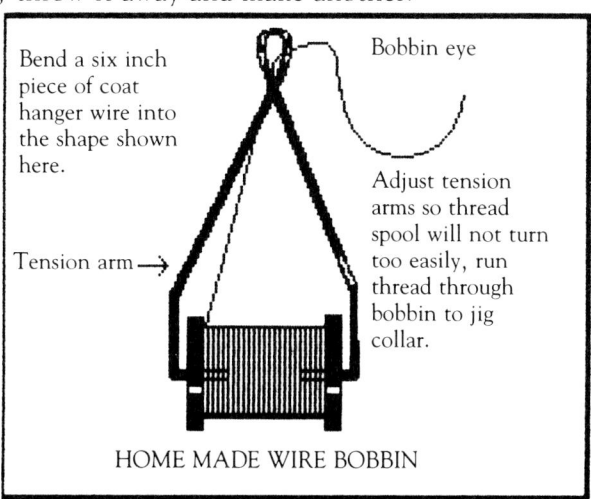

Homemade clothes hanger wire bobbin.

MAKING AND USING THE MARABU JIG

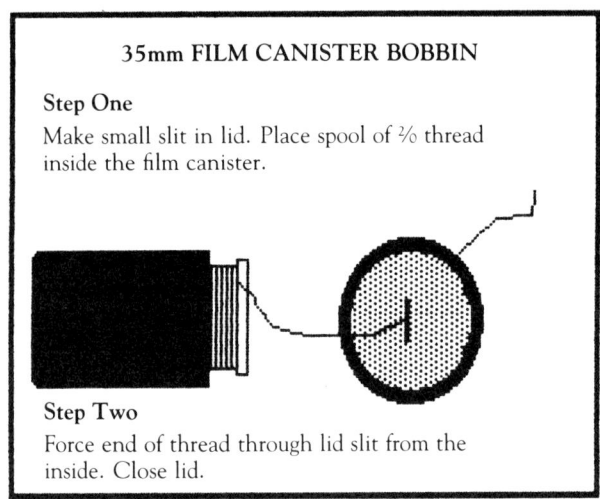

35mm FILM CANISTER BOBBIN

Step One
Make small slit in lid. Place spool of ⅔ thread inside the film canister.

Step Two
Force end of thread through lid slit from the inside. Close lid.

If you don't have one of these small film canisters on hand, most local film developing services will give you a few because they throw them out anyway.

5) **A FLY TYING VISE.** This is a one time investment which will cost upwards from about $ 8.00. Until you determine whether or not you will enjoy creating your own lures you can do an excellent job using the vise grip from your tool box. Straddle the vice grip's handles over the rim of a used, weighted coffee can and you've got an instant fly vise.

6) **SUPER GLUE FOR CEMENTING THE THREAD TO PREVENT UNRAVELING.**

7) **A SHARP PAIR OF FLY TYING SCISSORS; NO SUBSTITUTES!**

8) **PAINT.** There are three acceptable paints for coating jig heads: epoxy, lacquer, and vinyl. Epoxies and lacquers will eventually chip off the lure. Epoxy does last much longer than lacquer, but it's limited to black and white colors only. To date, epoxies have yet to develop a range of colors which are acceptable. Lacquers have the most dramatic and beautiful hues and are available in every color. Unfortunately, lacquer chips too easily.

Recently a new vinyl product has become available. It's chip resistant, has a variety of quality colors, and dries quickly. It was created specifically to paint lead jigs and can be found in most tackle shops.

With the above supplies on hand you're ready to start making some of the most effective fish-catching lures to hit the water.

FOUR EASY STEPS

1) **PAINTING THE HEADS:** You'll need to string a length of very small aluminum chain across an out-of-the-way, dust-free area. This will provide you with a place to hang the freshly painted lures. Using chain will keep the wet lures separated. If you use wire, the wet heads will slide together and stick as the wire sags in the center from the weight of the jigs. Try to use enough chain to accommodate 25 to 50 jigs.

Each jig head must first be painted with a coat of white and allowed to dry before coating with the actual color you want on the head. The undercoating of white is necessary to give the finish coat its brilliance. Dip the head of each lure into the paint and hang it up to dry. Don't forget to paint up a good supply of pink and black heads.

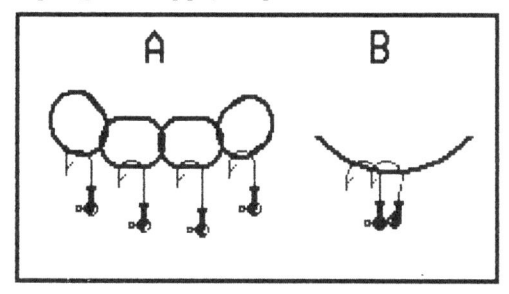

Unless the wet heads are prevented from touching (A), they'll slide and dry together (B).

2) **CLAMP AND THREAD THE HOOK:** Place the hook of the jig into the vice with the point hidden within the jaws of the vice. It's not necessary to hide the hook, but after you've stuck the hook point into your finger a few times, you'll appreciate its importance.

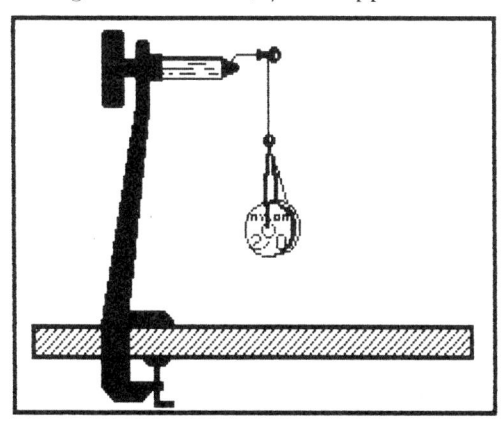

2/0 nylon thread has the strength to withhold the pulling pressure needed to firmly hold the marabou to the collar. The small 2/0 diameter leaves a smooth finish.

Next, wind about eight turns of red number 2/0 nylon thread around the collar of the jig. Each wind should cross over the previous one. This will prevent the thread from slipping from the collar without having to tie it into place. It takes a little practice to get the hang of this, but once you do, it will save you a lot of time. Otherwise, you might prefer to tie on the thread. The purpose of the thread is to hold the feathers to the collar, forming the body of the lure.

We use 2/0 thread because of its small diameter. Once the wrap is finished the thin line is noticeably smooth. The bulky rope-like wraps which result from larger diameter thread are too easily torn free by the constant snagging of crappie teeth, twigs, and anything else it rubs up against. Besides, the smoother wraps look better. Despite being thin, nylon is quite strong, which will allow for a very tight wrap around the collar without breaking the thread.

3) BUILDING THE BODY: The body of the lure is formed by tying marabou feathers to the collar. When you buy your marabou, go through them carefully, selecting only the most fluffy ones. Examine the barbs of each feather. Only those barbs which contain the thick fluffy barbules pictured on the right of page 31 should be used; those represented on the left must be discarded. Grasp several barbs with your thumb and first finger. Cut them from the main stalk (rachis) of the feather with your scissors.

Next, place the feathers on top of the collar, working the stems of the barbs around both sides, forming a hula skirt around the jig. Make sure the stems are pointing toward the head with the fluffy ends back over the hook.

Important: The lure from the tip of the lead head to the end of the feathers must not exceed one and one-half inches.

It's better to draw the stems up over the head and trim the excess at that point, rather than to trim the tail end. Should you trim the tail end, you will destroy most of the tail's ability to pulsate in a lifelike manner.

4) WRAP AND TIE THE FEATHERS IN PLACE: Make about 20 or 30 wraps of bobbin thread around the marabou stems and collar until the unsightly stems are no longer visible.

Take about an eight inch separate piece of thread and fold it in half, forming a four-inch loop. Place the loop parallel to the hook along the top of the collar with the loop forward. Wrap about nine or ten more turns over the loop.

Grasp the wrapped collar between your thumb and first finger. Cut the thread hanging from the collar to the bobbin one inch below the collar. Feed the one-inch end through the loop. Now pick up the two loose ends of the four-inch loop and jerk. The one-inch piece will

MAKING AND USING THE MARABU JIG

Only those fluffy feathers represented by the one on the right should be used.

Place the feathers on top of the collar, forming a hula skirt around the jig. The thread which is wound around the collar should be no wider than 1/16 inch.

·31·

be drawn under its own coils, holding it securely in place without a knot which can work lose causing the wrap to unravel. Trim the excess piece of thread and super glue the wrap. Congratulations! You now possess one of the most deadly crappie lures ever devised.

With a separate piece of thread, form a loop to place over the wrap. Add 9 or 10 more turns over the loop. :

Feed the collar wrap of thread through the loop and draw it beneath its own coils; trim.

FLY ROD STREAMERS AND TWO COLOR JIGS

Fly rod streamers can be made by going through the same procedure for tying jigs. Except you will want to use fly weight hooks. To get a pink head on your streamer you will have to paint the wrap itself pink after the super glue dries. To combine two tail colors on a streamer or a jig, simply tie on first one color using a little less feathers and make only a few turns of the collar wrap. Then add second color feathers on top of the first. Make your final wraps, and tie off.

OTHER COLORS

BLACK/GREEN AND YELLOW/GREEN

Sometimes crappies will spawn in and over very black vegetation or over black muddy bottoms. To make your black lure a little more noticeable you can add dark green to your black lures. When fishing these areas in early morning hours, it pays to use a dark green body with a yellow head. The yellow head is strictly for visibility; the green is an impressionistic model of a minnow. Most minnows have some olive green coloration.

These color combinations are among the author's favorites for catching crappies under almost all situations.

WHITE AND PINK/WHITE

In crystal clear lakes with little or no aquatic vegetation these colors are unbeatable. The pink/white is more easily seen by crappies in clear lakes with a very small amount of algal bloom. Whenever two-feather colors are combined, always put the lighter color on the bottom of the lure. Minnows are much lighter on their undersides.

There are times when white is also an outstanding color selection on lakes that are not very clear. If a lake has a heavy algal bloom, mid-morning and mid-afternoon sunlight will bounce off the nearly microscopic sized cells of algae, giving the water a greenish-yellow tinge. Yellow jigs, and to some extent pink/yellow jigs, are harder to see in such conditions. White will still be easily seen.

YELLOW

Yellow is an outstanding color even when used without pink. It is especially effective in tannin or tea-colored water where pink would too easily be camouflaged. In such water, the more yellow the better. It is recommended that the red-thread collar be maintained to create the impression of minnow gills. White crappies really like this color in turbid rivers and reservoirs.

PRESENTING YOUR LURE TO THE FISH

You've probably heard the expression that lures are made to catch fishermen not fish. There is probably a lot of truth to that. Over the years, tackle manufacturers have convinced most anglers that their lures must pop, fizz, spin, gurgle, or dance to be effective. And if the fisherman doesn't catch fish, he can at least enjoy watching the action of his lure. I've never seen a minnow pop, fizz or spin, and I really couldn't tell you if they gurgle or dance. Maybe they do so when the lights are low.

Nonetheless, action lures do catch most species of fish. But they aren't preferable for crappies, except maybe for the dancers. For a crappie lure to work, it simply has to be seen. And to be seen it has to be a very slow mover. In most situations the world of the crappie is cluttered with weeds, flooded timber, or other types of cover. Fast moving lures are too easily lost to crappies, which are relatively slow swimmers.

The function of action lure design is to entice fish to locate the lure and attack it. As you will discover when you crappie fish, you must locate the crappies rather than have them find you. And once you have found the fish or their hideouts, you just stick the bait or lure in their faces. They'll do the rest.

But sticking the lure in their face is an art in itself when you consider the places they might be hiding. Since crappies are found in different types of structure, different types of lure placements or presentations are needed.

CAST AND RETRIEVE

The method of fishing most commonly used by anglers is the cast and retrieve presentation. There is really nothing complicated about it, and it is accomplished just as its name implies; the lure is simply cast to a likely spot and the lure is very slowly retrieved and cast again. The key for success with this presentation is *slow movement.* You should retrieve so slowly that the lure barely moves.

Cast and retrieve is used mainly in open water situations where the angler needs to be at a distance from the fish so they cannot see him. It is also used to reach places too far away for the angler to approach. For example, a shore fisherman will use the cast and retrieve presentation to reach deeper water or to fish river eddies. This is most often the type of presentation that bobber fishermen use. Since minnows often move about in short darting motions, it sometimes helps to retrieve your lure with the same darting action, remembering to go slowly so you don't outrun the fish.

JIGGING OR YO-YOING

The word "jig" means to dance or bob up and down. As it applies to fishing it means to dance a lure up and down in a yo-yoing action. The lure is lowered to a place where crappies are located, and then the lure is raised and lowered repeatedly until a crappie takes the lure. The dancing or jigging motion can be in very short, slow jerks of four or five inch moves or raised as much as two or three feet at a time. The dancing motion is imparted to the lure to attract attention to it. It will appear to be a wounded minnow which will make an easy meal for the crappie to catch.

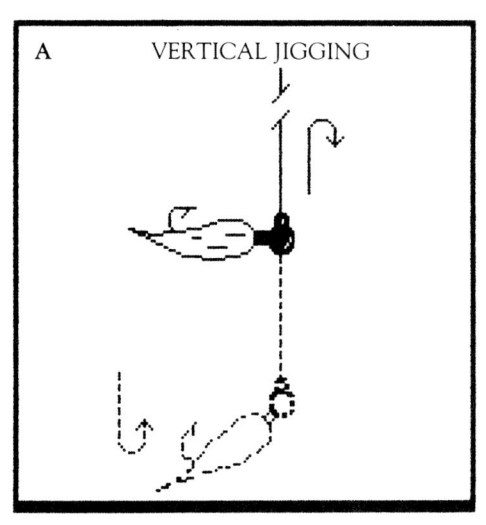

(A) In deep water jigs are fished by raising and lowering them to match the level where the fish are holding and also to draw attention.

```
┌─────────────────────────────────────────┐
│   B      CAST AND RETRIEVE JIGGING      │
│                                         │
│           (illustration)                │
└─────────────────────────────────────────┘
```

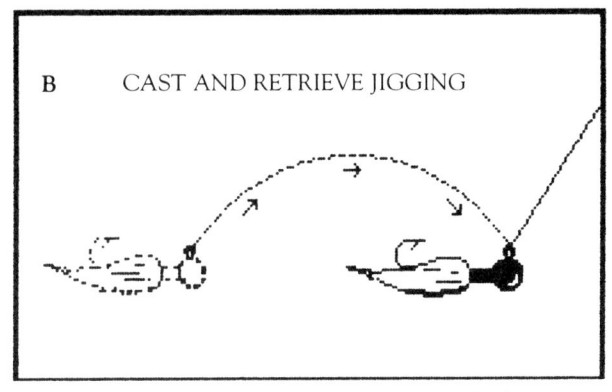

(B) Jigging action should be used when fishing with the cast-and-retrieve method in shallow water with a lot of stain, tint, or turbidity.

JIGGER-POLING OR POKE FISHING

By far the most productive timber and heavy vegetation technique for taking crappies is the jigger-pole. A jigger-pole rig is nothing more than a 10 to 12-foot cane pole with an added length of monofilament to which is tied a jig or hook and minnow. The rig is mainly used to reach back into areas where casting or retrieving is not possible because of over hanging limbs, heavy vegetation, or other obstruction that would prevent an angler from reaching a likely spot.

There is really nothing sophisticated about this type of presentation. The fishermen simply sticks the tip of the pole back into the area he wishes to fish and "pokes" the lure or bait into the water. Most anglers who use this method will fish with a minnow hanging about 2 feet below a bobber. Actually it's a variation of the old fashioned hook, line, sinker, and cane pole rig. It is deadly on crappies that are hiding in flooded timber or under floating cattails.

Because minnows aren't really necessary to catch crappies, I recommend that the bobber and hook be replaced by tying a jig directly to the line and just poking it into the target area. There is one problem with using a jig without a bobber. You're going to hang up quite a bit, but you will definitely catch crappies.

WIND DRIFTING AND SLOW TROLLING

Very simply, this consists of slowly moving your boat along with an electric trolling motor or allowing the wind to drift you along as you trail your bait or lure behind the boat at various depths. This can be an excellent way to locate isolated groups of suspended crappies. Usually when contact is made with fish, the angler drops a small marker buoy overboard to mark the location. He then positions himself next to the marker and fishes the entire area with the jigging technique.

TANDEM RIGGING (two lures on the same line)

When you are river fishing in open water at great depths and the crappies are holding in a specific spot near the bottom, you will want to get your lure back down to them as quickly as possible. This is especially important in rivers where even the slightest current can carry your lure away from the area where the fish are holding as the lure slowly descends. Some anglers add lead weights to their bait to get it back down in a hurry. But that's not very efficient. If you decide to add extra weight it might as well be an additional lure, which will increase your odds of catching fish. Heavier lures should be avoided if possible. It's better to use two ¹/₃₂ oz. jigs rather than one ¹/₁₆ ounce.

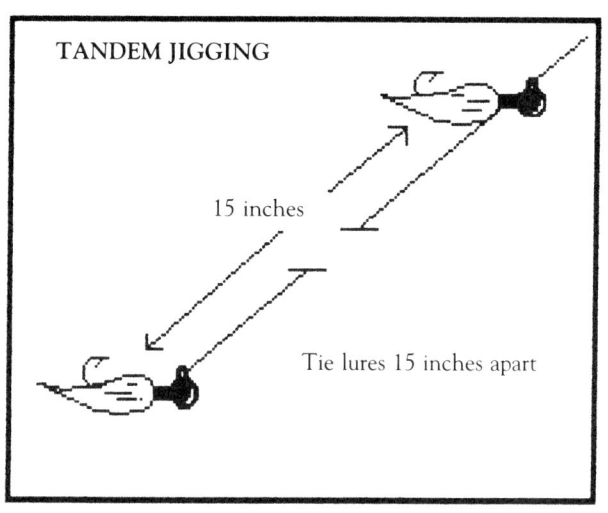

TANDEM JIGGING

15 inches

Tie lures 15 inches apart

¹/₃₂ ounce jigs fished in tandem are very effective in deep water, especially in rivers where the current can easily drift a single lightweight lure off target.

Many states do not allow anglers to have more than one hook on a line, at least in some of their waters. But if your state's laws permit, a very effective deep water presentation is the *tandem rig*. The tandem rig is created by tying two jigs on your line about 15 inches apart. Curiously, crappies will sometimes sit right on the bottom. At other times they will suspend about a foot above the bottom. With the tandem rig you are covering both depths and will increase your odds of catching fish. These rigs are fished by trolling, drifting, or jigging. Make sure the lower jig touches the bottom of the river or lake every few inches as you move along.

Unless your lure (or bait) is in the water it won't catch fish. Most anglers spend only about half their fishing day with their lure actually in the water.

A final thought about presenting your lure to crappies or any fish for that matter. Unless your lure (or bait) is in the water it won't catch fish. Of course you know this, but you would be surprised at the number of fishermen who do not put into practice this simple fact. After observing other anglers for years, I can tell you with certainty that most anglers only spend about half their fishing day with their lures actually in the water. The next time you go fishing, please make a special effort to observe your own habits. I think you will be amazed at the amount of time your lure is not in the water.

SETTING THE HOOK (SPEED NOT STRENGTH)

The joy of catching fish often quickly turns to anger and frustration when the fish gets off. Most experienced anglers know that just because a fish has taken their bait that does not mean that the fish has been hooked. To insure that the hook is stuck into the fish, the angler has to give the fishing line a good yank, which drives the hook into the mouth tissue of the fish. This is *"setting the hook."*

Because of the very thin tissue of the crappie's mouth, the hook must be set much more gently than with any other fish. If not, the very act of hooking the fish will also be the act of unhooking the fish because the lure might be torn free from the thin tissue. With crappies the most important thing to remember when setting the hook is to do it quickly. When fishing for walleyes with live bait or bass with plastic worms, anglers have learned to wait for a few seconds before setting the hook. With crappies this would be a critical mistake. You must move fast but gently.

If you properly hook a large crappie you will have a very worthy opponent on the other end of the line. Landing him will still be quite a challenge. In the next chapter we will explore the all important techniques for playing and landing your fish.

GIVE 'EM ENOUGH LINE AND THEY'LL HANG THEMSELVES

Okay! You've tied or purchased 20 or 30 marabou or plastic jigs and you're ready to jerk jaws. Right? Please hold on to your patience just a little longer. However miraculous marabou jigs might perform, they can't catch fish by themselves. There are just a few more things about fishing technique and tackle to discuss that will certainly increase your crappie catching ability when mastered.

FISHING LINE

For a week or so the crappie action had been fantastic on a small metropolitan lake near my Minnesota home. I decided to take a friend who was known, and of course appropriately teased, for his inability to catch fish. Since the crappies were always easy to find on this lake anyway, I figured I could help my buddy break his fishing jinx by taking him along.

Once we were on the water I was getting a hit on every cast; true to his form, my fishing partner wasn't doing as well. I was hooking eight or nine fish to his one. We were fishing from the same boat, casting to the same spot, and both using $1/32$ oz. marabou jigs of the same color on light spinning gear. So why wasn't he catching many crappies? What else could he be doing that was different? I stopped fishing for awhile and just watched him.

I noticed that my angling friend was making two very basic mistakes. First, he wasn't watching his fishing line. And second, his line was too heavy. Both were easily corrected. To his delight, he began to catch fish and has continued to catch crappies whenever he now goes fishing. (Now we just tease him about how small his fish are.)

BECOME A LINE WATCHER

Many anglers will automatically snap a bobber on their lines when fishing for crappies, whether they're using live bait or casting small lures. And under certain conditions which will be discussed later, bobbers are helpful. Usually they are not. Crappie anglers should fish bobberless 95% of the time. Such was the case with my fishless friend and me. We were simply casting our jigs and slowly retrieving them without a bobber on the line.

Crappie anglers should fish bobberless 95% of the time.

Most anglers who fish without bobbers rely almost exclusively on the telltale taps they feel telegraphed up their fishing lines when a fish bites and tugs on their bait or lure. Those who rely only on these taps, however, are missing a lot of fish. Actually, a crappie fisherman will not feel a fish tap on the line about four out of every five times. Often fish will spit lures back out without pulling on them, or they might take the presentation so gently that detection isn't possible.

An alert angler will learn to watch his fishing line (and his lure in really clear water) as faithfully as he would a bobber and will be able to tell if a fish has grabbed his lure, even if he doesn't feel a tap. In crystal clear water I've observed crappies engulf my lures many times, and only on occasion would I feel a tap.

LOOK FOR LIMPNESS (OR A TWITCH IN THE LINE)

Usually, when a crappie takes its prey it does so from behind and underneath. As you retrieve your lure if you see your line suddenly twitch and go limp, a crappie has just taken your lure from below and behind. The crappie is swimming up and toward you. When it overtakes the lure, it actually creates a bit of slack for a split second because it was swimming in your direction faster than the lure was moving. Before it spits the lure out, you have to set the hook because fish do not automatically become hooked when they ingest a lure. Only if the crappie turns back with its prize is it likely to hook itself, as it tugs against your line while holding on to the lure or bait.

There is another situation in which crappies will cause your line to go slack and you will never feel their presence. It happens often when jigging directly below your boat in deep water or when you are ice fishing. As you raise and lower the jig to draw the crappies' attention to it or to make sure you are at the proper depth, crappies will sometimes swim upward to seize the lure as it drops back.

As a crappie swims up to meet the jig, it will grab the lure in "mid water" much like a dog will jump up for a ball in mid air. For a few seconds the crappie will suspend at the depth where he took the lure. Not realizing that a fish is holding on to your jig, you will continue to lower your rod tip to allow the lure to sink. But the lure can't sink since the crappie has it in his mouth. The line between the crappie and the rod tip will go slack, developing a big bend or bow in it. When you see this, snap your rod tip upwards immediately to hook the fish.

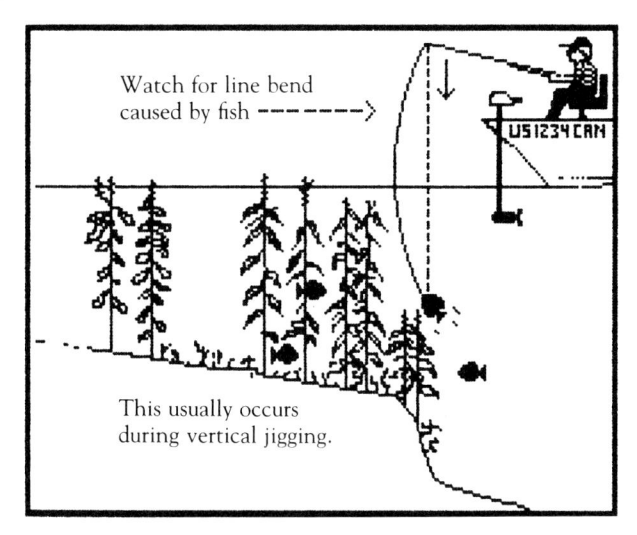

Watch for line bend caused by fish -------->

This usually occurs during vertical jigging.

If your line goes slack too soon to be resting on the bottom, set the hook! A crappie has probably grabbed it on the way down.

WATCH FOR MOVEMENT TO ONE SIDE

Sometimes your line will take off to one side or the other. A crappie ambushing your lure from the side might continue to swim in the same direction of its attack after it has swallowed the intended victim. As it does so, it will cause your line to move sideways in the water. Should you see your line move to the side set the hook.

It takes a little self discipline at first to remember to watch for your line to go limp or travel sideways in the water. But becoming a line watcher is an important ingredient to becoming a better crappie angler. Once you are aware of its importance and practice it, watching will become instinctive.

SMALLER FISHING LINES CATCH MORE FISH

This was the second basic mistake that my fishing partner had made. I asked to see his fishing line and discovered that he was using 10 lb. test line; I was using 4 lb. test. Since a good crappie fisherman has to watch his line, one might think that the line should be fairly large in size to make it easier to see. Nothing is further from the truth. One of the most difficult ideas to convince some anglers is that *smaller lines catch more fish.*

Heavy test line is easily seen by fish and tends to distract them. However, if you're fishing right down in heavy brush where the line won't be noticeable, heavy test line isn't so bad and you'll save a lot of lures.

But we were fishing in open water retrieving our lures through the tops of pondweed where there was little concealment for our lines. To a crappie, that 10 lb. test line must have looked like a phone pole does to us. The whole purpose of using artificial lures is to imitate live organisms which crappies feed upon. A small lure with relatively large bulky line attached is not very realistic in appearance. Ironically, there are times when heavy test monofilament line can magnify light and produce its own minnow-imitating flash which might distract a crappie from its intended target. I have observed fish approach fishing line and actually peck at it.

Despite not catching fish until he replaced his heavy line, my friend had performed a near olympic feat by casting a 1/32 oz. jig on such thick heavy monofilament. It's nearly impossible to cast light jigs for any distance or with accuracy using such heavy line.

Understandably, anglers are afraid of breaking off their lures on snags or larger fish, so they use heavy line. But the end result is worse than losing a lure. You get fewer bites in the first place, and quite often because of the lack of sensitivity in heavier line you aren't aware of many of the strikes you might get.

Smaller diameter line will telegraph the taps of a fish to you much better than the heavier, more shock-absorbent line. The tap you feel may be the fish grabbing the feathers or even the lead-head. The taps are generated by the tug on the line as the fish turns. Most of the time they will stop, taste the lure, then spit it out, if the marabou hasn't snagged their gills or teeth.

When the water is crystal clear, you don't need to feel the tap. Just set the hook when you see the fish grab it. But when your lure is not in your sight or when your line watching isn't paying off, those taps become all-important.

You should insure as much sensitivity as possible by using the smaller diameter test lines. With ordinary monofilament the best weight line for accuracy, distance, sensitivity, and realism with these ultra-light lures is 4 lb. test.

Try to get used to the idea that you are going to lose a few lures on snags with lighter lines. It's a fair trade for the number of fish you will catch. And it's another reason to make your own lures. You save money, have the colors you want, and always have plenty of spares.

What about losing big fish on 4 lb. line? Can't slab crappies break such thin lines? Not at all! At least it won't if you have taken good care of your line. If you should find a lake or river with crappies that break 4 lb. line, send me the location and your address. I'll treat you to a steak dinner after the fishing trip, providing my heart withstands the excitement.

Of course crappies aren't the only "fish in the sea." If you aren't bothered by the prospect of tying into bass, northern pike, walleyes, or whatever else might be lurking beneath your boat, be assured that light line will keep you busy. If you are fishing water that's particularly infested with northerns, you will lose a few lures to bite offs. But northern pike bite offs can occur no matter what test line you use.

Anglers lose fish for three reasons: 1) their lines break because they weren't taken care of; 2) the fish weren't hooked well to begin with because the hook wasn't set hard enough; 3) some fish simply tear the hook from their flesh and escape.

The main link between you and those crappies is your fishing line. It is the single most important physical item of your fishing gear.

You should handle your fishing line with care bordering on fanaticism. The greatest lure in the world means very little if you can't land your fish because your line breaks.

LINE BREAKAGE IS ALMOST ALWAYS PREVENTABLE

If your line is properly maintained, you will have little trouble with breakage. The following steps will be helpful:
1) Use high quality brand name monofilament.
2) Never allow boat battery acid, heat, or sharp objects to touch your line. (You can't do much about pike teeth.)
3) Never leave your line in the trunk of a car or inside any vehicle with the windows rolled up. The heat will destroy the line.
4) If you snag your hook and excessively stretch your line, check it carefully for splinter-like roughness. If it is not perfectly smooth, replace it. It will have lost most of its strength.
5) Lubricate your knots with a drop of saliva or water as you tie them. Then slowly draw them up tight, thus preventing friction. If you've ever received a rope burn playing tug of war, you can easily see how friction can generate enough heat to destroy a knot made of soft plastic.

   ALWAYS USE THE CLINCH KNOT. The clinch knot is made by first passing the line through the eye of the jig hook about four inches. Next, wind the line end around the main line exactly seven turns. Bring the line end through the small loop formed just above the hook eye as shown. Draw the knot up tightly and trim the excess line.

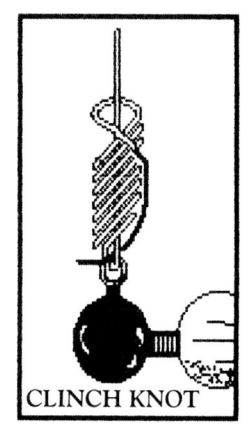

CLINCH KNOT

6) Test your knot and line after each fish and retie it about every fifth crappie.
7) Retie your knot at the beginning of each fishing day. The knot has some natural stress to it and will weaken overnight.
8) Protect your line from prolonged exposure to direct sunlight. The ultraviolet rays will weaken it.
9) Make sure your reel has the proper drag setting.

PLAYING A CRAPPIE: THE KEY TO LANDING YOUR FISH

By far you will lose more crappies which tear the hook free from their flesh than you will by your line breaking or by failing to set the hook properly.

Crappies are notorious for tearing free. When you examine the tissue-thin makeup of the crappie's mouth, you will see that it's a marvel they can be landed at all. After you've hooked a crappie you must play him with the finesse worthy of any trout. The bigger the crappie, the more delicate you will have to be. His weight alone will tear the hook free from the thin mouth tissue if you are too forceful.

Even though you mustn't be too forceful, you will have to keep a slight steady pressure on the fish. Even then, some tearing of the mouth tissue is inevitable. All it takes is a small tear in the tissue and a hook will easily become dislodged and fall free. If you give crappies any slack at all, you might as well say goodbye to them.

The mouth tissue is easily torn. Never give a crappie slack line or the hook can easily fall out.

If you set your drag lightly it will prevent you from tearing the hook free from the thin mouth and greatly reduce the tearing of the tissue. A lightly set drag also prevents the loss of very large fish, whatever the species.

The most important consideration to remember when playing any fish is to keep it hooked at the end of your line. Concentrate more on playing the fish to keep it hooked than on landing it.

As obvious as it might sound, keeping a fish hooked is the last thing on many anglers' minds when the thrill of hooking a fish takes over. They excitedly reel the fish toward them, thinking only of landing it. After all, isn't that why they're fishing? Indeed, it is. But the very excitement of trying hurriedly to land big crappies accounts for a large number of lost fish and colorful language. Please make this your first priority once you've hooked a fish: Concentrate more on playing a fish to keep it hooked than on landing it.

Successful crappie anglers must have a keen sense of balance, maintaining just enough applied pressure to keep the fish coming in, while never giving slack. Crappies are not known for long runs, but large ones are capable of quite a fight and will make powerful short runs. This is where most big slab-sided crappies are lost. Don't force them in.

You can overcome the effect of the short run by lowering both the rod and your arm toward the fish as it moves away, keeping just a little pressure on the fish. But do so only enough to accommodate the run, never allowing the line to go slack. When the fish runs in your direction, take up the slack by raising your rod and slowly reeling him in. As long as you keep the fish hooked you will eventually land it. Again, make sure your drag is set lightly.

You should always use a landing net on large crappies because their own weight can tear them free from the hook.

SPINNING EQUIPMENT: THE CRAPPIE DOOMSDAY MACHINE

There are three basic types of casting reels: spinning, spin-casting, and bait-casting. I would like the crappie fisherman to seriously consider the merits of using the spinning reel.

Bait-casting reels are primarily for use with large lures and bait which are used to pursue very large fish such as pike or trophy bass.

Spin-cast reels (or closed face as they are sometimes called) are the most popular reels among children and novice fishermen. They're usually trouble free, easy to cast, and never backlash. Unfortunately, due to their design they create a considerable amount of resistance to outflowing line, making it nearly impossible to cast ultralight $\frac{1}{32}$ oz. jigs with them.

Hook setting can also be a problem with several models of spin-cast reels. Inside the cover of many models is a small catch pin which retracts when cast and pops out again as line is reeled in. The pin's purpose is to catch the line and spin it around the spool to draw the line onto the reel. Occasionally with light lures, the coils of the spooled fishing line will slip over the pin and out of the reel. The result can be very disappointing if this happens just as you are about to set the hook. Instead of hooking a fish, line simply peals off the spool and out of the reel.

Probably the biggest problem with a spin-casting reel is its location on the rod. Spin-cast rods are designed so that the reels are mounted on the top of the rod forward of the hand grip; whereas, spinning reels are mounted beneath the rod and slightly behind the center of the hand grip.

The significance of this has to do with balance and sensitivity. It is absolutely essential for the angler to develop his/her sense of touch or sensitivity so sharply that even the slightest change in pressure on the fishing line can be detected.

A fishing rod becomes an extension of your line and serves as a feeler gauge, telegraphing every bump and tap from a fish to your hand. Because the spin-cast reel is forward of your hand, it adds a considerable amount of weight to the front of your rod, greatly reducing its balance. An unbalanced rod and reel outfit with excess forward weight will physically prevent the angler from being able to detect the lighter taps on his line.

Because spinning equipment is almost always balanced, your equipment will maintain the ability to telegraph vibrations. Furthermore, the weight of the reel hanging beneath the rod and behind your hand helps you raise the rod tip faster. This counterweight gives you additional speed and power when setting the hook.

Finally, spinning rods and reels are designed to be held with your strong hand, which also gives you an added advantage of a faster reflex action for setting the hook. Spin-cast outfits by contrast are held with your weak hand. So naturally, the reflexes needed to rapidly set the hook aren't as great.

The best spinning reels are those which have no resistance at all when the handle is turned. So, any resistance that you do feel while retrieving your lure is probably a fish. And crappie anglers should never select a spinning reel which has a clicking feeling as the handle turns. These clicks will distract your attention from those all important taps from a fish's strike. Distracting reel clicks will be indistinguishable from telltale fish taps.

When choosing a spinning rod, I believe that graphite rods are preferable to fiberglass, though they are more costly. Sensitivity is the key reason. Graphite telegraphs vibrations more intensely than does fiberglass. In most situations I've found the little ultralight rods to be the most satisfactory for conducting messages from our finny friends below. And the ultralight flexibility has just enough give to prevent crappies from tearing away from the hook in most cases.

While I strongly recommend ultralight rods, *I do not recommend ultralight reels.* After line has been on a spool for some time, it will develop what is known as "memory." Line will take on the shape or memory of the spool it's wound around. As you let out a few feet of line from its spool, it will form into coils.

Line which has been wound around ultralight spools will develop a memory (or shape) of small coils; large spools develop large coils. Tiny spools of ultralight reels cause a given length of monofilament line to form twice as many coils as it would on a regular-sized reel.

Because of the tendency of coils to resist straightening out, they create resistance as the line feeds through the rod guides, cutting down on the distance and accuracy of your cast. Since there are more coils coming from an ultralight reel than from a larger one, there is also more resistance. This becomes quite crucial in cold weather when monofilament becomes very stiff; casting can be nearly impossible!

In addition to making more accurate casts at a greater distance, larger reels will hold more line. Occasionally, you will break your line. With larger spools you will have a ready supply of extra line at hand.

It's not a good idea to retie line which has broken off. First of all, it has been weakened by whatever broke it in the first place. Secondly, you will create a bumpy knot within the casting length of the retied piece which I guarantee will snag your line every other time you cast, causing you to invent new words. The extra spool capacity you will gain will insure an ample supply of line, so you won't have to retie your broken piece. I have found it helpful to pack along an extra pre-spooled line for each reel just in case I lose a lot of line. If you find that you absolutely must retie your line, don't anyway!

You should always use top grade monofilament. There is no need, however, to fill your entire spool with expensive 4 lb. mono. You can fill your spool halfway with any backing that might be handy then join your best line to it to fill the spool. Again, do not use a knot to join the lines or you will create that bumpy snag. Overlap the two ends ½ inch and super glue them. Then finish filling your spool with the higher quality line.

Do not join your fishing line ends with knots when adding additional line to your spool. Overlap them and apply a drop of super glue.

Please make every effort to retrieve your broken line. Discarded line can be devastating to birds or other creatures which entangle themselves in it. If there is such a thing as a fishing sin, one would be to violate the following rule:

Thou shalt not discard fishing line anywhere but in a trash receptacle, and only then after you have cut it into small three or four inch pieces.

Once you have assembled your ultralight spinning rod with a normal sized spinning reel, loaded it with high grade 4 lb. test line, and tied on a $\frac{1}{32}$ oz. marabou jig, you will command one of the most effective crappie catching implements ever devised. Additionally, two other types of poles are valuable to the crappie angler: a telescoping pole which extends to 10 or 12 feet and a small 3 foot jig stick. Their uses will be discussed later.

From Bobber to Basket

BOBBERS

While a bobber can be a useful tool for the angler, there may be no single piece of fishing equipment that is misused more.

One Saturday, while I was checking shore fishermen, I came to a fellow sitting about a hundred yards from a culvert that joined two lakes. The man was fishing with a minnow hanging a few feet below a bobber. I had noticed that he would catch a crappie only once in a good while.

Anglers fishing nearer the culvert were having a great time catching fish. I let him know that he could improve his luck if he moved closer to the culvert, took his bobber off, and jigged his minnow up and down at different depths. He gave me a very serious look and responded, "Oh no! I don't want to do that. If I catch my limit too soon I'll have to go home. Then my wife'll put me to work around the house." This corny but true story illustrates an important point about the uses and misuses of bobbers.

To this fellow it didn't matter if he caught fish. He was just there to relax, kill time, and escape his wife's housecleaning detail. Most anglers do want to catch at least some fish, and yet many of them unknowingly defeat their own efforts fishing just the way this fellow had been, by using (of all things) bobbers.

How on earth can a bobber keep you from catching fish? Surely, the main reason most anglers use bobbers is to tell them that a fish has taken their bait. In fact, one of the most popular ways of fishing is to hook a minnow below a bobber, cast out as far as possible hoping that the minnow doesn't sling off the hook, and then just sit back on a lawn chair or your boat seat waiting for the bobber to be pulled under. It's relaxing and an easy way to fish, but it is likely the worst.

If the bobber doesn't go under after a long, frustrating wait, the line is eventually reeled in, the bait checked, and perhaps the fishing depth changed. The rig is then cast back out and the wait for the bobber to disappear starts all over again. Unfortunately, this method of bobber fishing, with a few exceptions, is overall the least effective way to catch crappies.

BOBBER PROBLEMS

VISIBILITY: You must pay constant attention to a bobber to effectively use it. By far, the bobber that seems most popular with anglers is the spherical plastic model which is red on the bottom and white on top. Frankly, I cannot understand its popularity. You have to strain your eyes to see the white top in the reflective water. And when fishing it in rivers, near areas where incoming streams, dams, or fast water creates white foam, you can't see it at all. During the ice fishing season, white topped bobbers look too much like the snow and ice and can't be easily seen. Fluorescent orange or yellow bobbers are much easier to see.

Fluorescent orange or yellow bobbers are the most easily seen, especially during low light hours.

LOSS OF SENSITIVITY: The most negative thing about bobber fishing is the immediate loss of sensitivity. A bobber becomes a shock absorber and you simply will not feel those changes in line pressure so essential for detecting strikes. All you feel is the bobber.

LIMITING COVERAGE OF PRODUCTIVE WATERS: Most of the time, you will need the freedom to fish various depths. A bobber will prevent this because with it you are limited to a specific depth. Without a bobber you can cover much more water at different levels a lot faster with your lure or bait.

LINE DAMAGE: Another disadvantage to using a bobber is the damage that can occur to your fishing line by clamping a bobber to it. Even if you use the soft styrofoam bobbers which are held in place on the line with a small wooden peg, you will pinch the line with the peg and weaken it.

DISTRACTING TO FISH: I have actually had fish attack my bobber instead of going for the lure. Sometimes fish think bobbers are insects or some other small creature struggling on the surface of the water. The bobber's movement distracts the fish away from bait or lures.

A bobber can be a valuable tool and has its place in the tackle box. The angler that is selective in using one in the right situations will certainly increase his/her catch of crappies.

For those who insist on using them, it should be noted that using a bobber to tell if fish are biting is only one of its helpful uses. The following helpful hints will be useful: They are also used to control fishing depth, to cast long distances, and to give action to lures and to help to set the hook.

DEPTH CONTROL

As we discuss actual fishing techniques in later chapters we will more thoroughly cover the best way to use a bobber for depth control. However, it will be instructive to briefly list the following three uses.

TO PREVENT SINKING: In the spring of the year, especially in northern states just after ice out, crappies will hit only the slowest moving targets. When crappies are in very shallow water (2 to 4 feet) it's essential to use a bobber to prevent the lead head marabou jig from sinking to the bottom as you barely move the lure ever so slowly through the water.

If you don't have a bobber, you can prevent sinking, somewhat, by holding the rod tip very high as you reel the jig toward you. However, it will be extremely difficult to reel slowly enough to please the crappies. Using a bobber allows you to keep the lure off the bottom and almost at a standstill.

AS A DEPTH MARKER: During the winter months, crappies are likely to suspend at specific depths just as they will during the hot summer and for the same reasons: temperature comfort. Once you've located fish, a bobber helps you mark and maintain that level.

TO SAVE LURES: Except when crappies are actually on their nests, they will frighten quite easily. If you know crappies are in shallow water structures, but aren't spawning, you will have to cast to them from a distance to keep from spooking them. If there happens to be flooded timber or other snags in those spots, you will usually lose some jigs. Some of your losses can be cut by fishing your lure below a bobber fairly shallow, until you have determined that there are no snags or fish to be caught at that level. You can then drop your lure another foot or so below the bobber and try again.

DISTANCE CASTING AND HOOK SETTING

A bobber (still commonly called a cork in some parts of the country) is quite helpful to shore fishermen that need extra weight to get their light weight lures or bait out to deeper water. It's especially helpful to children who haven't developed the motor skills necessary for handling a spinning rod.

On windy days "corks" bob up and down on the wavy water causing the marabou lure hanging below to dance up and down sending an enticing lifelike message to nearby alert crappies. Often this bobbing will have the same effect as the angler setting the hook. Crappies will hook themselves if they engulf a jig just as the wave action jerks the bobber upward. But not every crappie which grabs a lure or bait beneath a bobber is going to hook itself.

It is very important to keep the slack out of your line when bobber fishing. The time it takes to reel in the slack so you can set the hook is quite often all the time a crappie needs to spit the lure out.

STRINGERS

I feel very strongly that stringers should be used only to hold fish up to take pictures. And then only on those fish which are NOT going to be released. I have seen so many nice catches of strung fish ruined by their having been dragged over stumps, limbs, rocks, or crushed between the bottom of the boat and whatever it comes into contact with.

Usually strung fish are hanging immediately beneath the water line on the side of the boat. Even if the fish aren't beat to pieces by objects in the water, the sun takes its toll on them. The direct heat of the sun on a fish held only inches below the surface of the water is deadly because of the water's surface temperature.

Because crappies don't have eye lids, those that are not shaded will be blinded by strong direct sunlight. Should some of the fish be released, they have been placed at a considerable disadvantage. Conscientious anglers will agree that there is no cause to torture fish with blindness or by grinding them against objects in the water. It is quite wasteful and disrespectful of a beautiful natural resource to treat fish this way.

Another problem with stringers, which is more common than most anglers realize, is the lack of protection your catch has from other "beasts" lurking in the water. Snapping turtles are notorious for robbing stringers. You can imagine the surprise and disappointment of an angler who wishes proudly to show off his catch, but upon lifting the stringer from the water finds a snapping turtle or some other creature polishing off his fish.

I must emphasize that anglers should not feel bad about using a stringer if they are displaying fish for taking photos or if they know for certain that they will keep every fish that goes on the stringer. If a stringer is your only option, your fish can still be kept fresh and in a humane manner. Tie a length of rope to the stringer and lower your

This strung fish had no protection from the viselike jaws of the hungry snapper.

fish into very deep water to keep your catch from the harsh sunlight. Please remember to check the condition of the fish frequently.

Rather than threading a stringer through a crappie's gills and mouth which is the common practice, a crappie is more easily strung by running the stringer through the bottom of the thin mouth tissue on the lower mandible and out through the mouth. This will allow the crappie the freedom to move water across its gills. The stringer does not have to go through its gill slits at all. Damage is done to the crappies' gills by running a stringer through them, greatly restricting the intake of oxygen. This is not quite as bad of a problem in early spring when the water is cold and keeps its oxygen better. But in warmer water the fish will slowly die.

Fish that are allowed to die slowly on a stringer, or for that matter under any condition, will lose much of their fresh flavor or even be completely ruined. If you can't keep them alive, you can insure their maximum freshness by placing them directly into a cooler with ice after promptly removing their gills and entrails. This will prevent bacterial growth or enzyme action from ruining your catch.

Without a live well, a wire mesh basket is an excellent way to protect your fish and keep them alive.

LIVE WELLS, WIRE BASKETS, AND PAILS

The best way to protect your catch and keep them alive and fresh is in an aerated live well. Not everyone can afford this option. So the next best thing is a wire mesh basket draped with a burlap bag for shade. The fish can freely and safely swim about inside while the burlap keeps the harshness of the sun from them. If you are fishing in a boat, please remember to keep the basket on the shaded side of the boat if you have no shading cover for the basket.

If a wire mesh basket is not an available option either, many crappie anglers have found large pickle pails quite handy to keep their fish in. These pails also make excellent seats for shore and ice fishermen. But you will have to change the water often to keep the fish fresh.

Now you're ready to head for the water and wet a line. You have made several marabou jigs, topped off your spinning reel with four pound test line and have at least picked up a five gallon pail to hold all your fish.

Well, that's about it for the basic tackle that you will need as I take you to some of my favorite fishing holes. There are a few other things that will be helpful from time to time such as polarized sunglasses, contour maps, and a few other conveniences which we will discuss later... as for now? You are ready to go fishing. You have everything ready from a good supply of marabou jigs to a basket to put your fish in. Now have you forgotten anything?

OOPS! DON'T FORGET YOUR FISHING LICENSE.

"Look Out Below, Crappies!"

Have you ever found crappies in a certain location on one fishing trip but weren't able to find them there the next time you went? Where did they go? Why weren't they still there? What caused them to move?

Just as predictably as a bear will hibernate and a duck will fly south for the winter, a crappie will also yield to the power of changes in nature's seasons and follow a prescribed pattern of behavior. As the seasons change the crappies' behavior changes. These changes are usually characterized by movement from one location to another for purposes of spawning, safety, comfort, or feeding. Fish movement is also greatly affected by the daily rhythm of daylight and darkness, especially for feeding.

The detailed patterns of crappie movement behavior in the following chapters will confirm this single most important fact about crappie fishing:

To be an effective crappie angler you must be willing to change constantly your fishing locations.

There is a lake in my patrol area that always seems to have a number of people fishing on its west shoreline. The lake is within view of a major freeway and has a gravel road running alongside, allowing easy access. Yet, I've never seen anyone with more than one or two small fish in possession, and even that is a rare occurrence. I've seen as high as 40 people at a time along that ¼ mile stretch, most fishless. Many of them will sit on the bank for hours without moving.

Why do they go there if there's no fish to be caught? Simply because they saw others fishing there as they drove along the freeway. With few exceptions, most would explain that they figured the spot must have good fishing because they would almost always see someone there. Actually, the lake is excellent for fishing if you have a boat, but it's an extremely shallow lake for several hundred feet out from shore, making shore fishing an unproductive prospect.

Using a boat doesn't guarantee success either. Most of my spring and summer work is spent in a boat checking fishing licenses and limits. One day while working on one of my largest lakes, I counted 15 boats anchored in an area so small I could hardly get my conservation boat between them. Not a single boat had fish. Most of the fishermen would ask me for recommendations on where else they might fish since this spot hadn't worked out. Many explained that they had seen other boats there and figured it had to be a good spot.

Interestingly, these anglers were closer in theory to catching fish than many I meet on the water. Many anglers have the idea that water plus fishing equipment equals fish. Certainly there is much more to fishing than that. Those anglers that figured they'd catch fish where they observed others fishing, at least had the knowledge that some locations will produce fish, whereas, others won't. This is a basic fundamental truth that must be clearly understood to successfully fish crappies:

Crappies have specific preferences for certain locations in any given body of water. Furthermore, there is a relationship between where crappies are located and the season of the year.

Three weeks earlier each of the 15 boats mentioned above could have limited out on crappies in the same place where they now found themselves fishless. Having given up, some of the boaters resignedly stated that they guess the fish just weren't biting today. Actually, the crappies had simply changed locations.

SOME CRAPPIES ARE ALWAYS BITING

The idea that crappies aren't biting on a given day is just a myth. There are always some crappies biting somewhere in any lake. You just have to find them. If you find that you aren't catching fish, please convince yourself that they just aren't at the location where you're fishing. Even if they were there, and not biting, then you might as well be somewhere else anyway. You simply must move about and find those that will bite.

CRAPPIE FISHING IS ACTUALLY A FORM OF HUNTING

Fishing should be considered an act of hunting. This cannot be overemphasized. A crappie angler's number one enemy when boat fishing can be his boat anchor. Every season I see hundreds of boats leave the boat ramps or resorts and fish camps, head out to some hopeful spot, and then drop anchor without first knowing if there are fish in the area. Even if the fish aren't there the temptation to stay put can be pretty strong. Sure, it's inconvenient to have constantly to pull up anchor and move about, but if a fisherman is willing to spend the time looking around, the following suggestions will assist him in locating crappies.

PROCEDURE FOR LOCATING CRAPPIES

There are four basic procedures for locating crappies. And none of these are exclusively separate from the others. You may find that at any one time you probably will be using two or three of them.

1) **WATCH OTHER ANGLERS.** Just don't follow them. If you observe fish being caught on a certain type of structure look for similar structures to fish. But please don't anchor down until you determine if fish are being caught. To promote courtesy when you are fishing open stretches of water, please leave some distance between yourself and other fishermen, unless you have their permission to come in close. If you are polite and ask respectfully, most anglers will welcome your company.

2) **ASK SOMEONE.** On larger lakes there is usually someone coming into boat launches at all hours. Most people will tell you where they caught their fish. Make sure you ask what depth they were fishing. Generally, crappies will be at the same depths throughout a lake.

Dealers in bait shops and fish camps are excellent sources of information on where to find crappies. I have found many excellent fishing holes this way. If you should locate fish, make sure you return the courtesy of stopping back by or phoning the bait shop to and thank the dealer. Share the details of your catch. You will find him cooperative in the future, and your tips will help other anglers.

3) **SEARCH FOR THEM IN SHALLOW WATER THROUGH POLARIZED SUNGLASSES.** In the spring, from nearly ice out to the end of spawning, with some exceptions, you can see crappies swimming about in clear shallow water if you are wearing sunglasses with polarized lenses.

Polarized sunglasses eliminate nearly all the reflection of the sun from the surface of the water, allowing you to see into the water. Even on cloudy days there will still be a certain amount of surface glare which must be eliminated. During the spring spawning season, very slowly wade or drift your boat through the shallows wearing these special sunglasses. You will actually be able to see crappies on their "beds." So the sun does not bounce off the inside of your sunglasses into your eyes you will have to wear a cap or hat with a large brim or visor.

4) **FINALLY, AND MOST IMPORTANT, YOU SHOULD FISH KNOWN CRAPPIE STRUCTURE.** Structure is one of those terms that fishermen have come to use which more or less sums up the when's and where's of fish movement. Structure might be a muddy bottom for a while, then four weeks later a sandy one. It can be a fallen dead tree or a clump of pondweed. Crappies appear to like each other's company, and when you find one at a certain structure, you are likely to find several others in the immediate area. This is partly due to the crappies' fondness for each other, but is primarily caused

by the forces of nature that drive them instinctively to prefer the same structure.

The following text will explain the marvelous varieties of crappie structure and how to fish them. As you look at structure please note:

In any given season, if you find crappies around a certain type of structure in one section of a lake, you are sure to locate them at identical structures in other parts of that lake.

CANALS, MUDDY BAYS WITH CATTAILS, AND CONNECTING PONDS

As the ice on northern lakes begin to thaw with the warming April weather and the earth responds in preparation for the miracles of spring, crappies begin to crowd into shallow water by the hundreds. The winter snows have now left the land, but ice still remains on the lakes. The rays of the sun are more easily absorbed by the dark earth surrounding the lake than by the reflecting white glassy iced surface of the lake itself. This causes the shoreline to melt first, as the earth around the rim of the lake becomes a great solar collector slowly heating the lake's edge.

Once the ice breaks away from shore and begins to recede, the rays of the sun penetrate the shallow water, heating the earth beneath the water's edge and accelerating the thawing process of the lake. It's shallow in areas such as channels, canals, and shallow muddy cattail bays, and small connecting ponds are the first to thaw.

These are the areas where winter-weary anglers really catch the crappies. I believe that more crappies are caught per day during this short two to three-week period than during any other comparable time of the year.

Some shallow areas will warm up faster than others, depending on the make up of the lake bottom. Light sandy areas will not store heat to the same degree as dark mucky bottoms. Dark mucky bottoms are usually found in areas where the dead remains of last year's cattails ring the edge of a lake or pond. But dark bottoms are also found in canals where silting from surrounding lands have deposited dark soil. Canals, ponds, and bays all support a variety of vegetation types. During the winter these plants die back and decompose further, depositing a treasure of dark-colored decayed organic substance, which readily absorbs and holds the sun's heat.

These areas are extremely fertile and sustain an interesting variety of aquatic life. The warmth of the spring sun causes them to explode with lifeforms which have been fairly dormant throughout the winter. As this happens, crappies move into these areas for about two to three weeks, although the peak of this movement will last only about 10 days.

Crappies leave the safety of deeper water and seek the shallows during this time to take advantage of the emerging abundance of insect and bait fish, which are in turn feeding on the increasing mass of plankton. Furthermore, temperature-sensitive crappies prefer the warmer shallows to the still near-freezing temperatures throughout the rest of the lake. The first crappies to appear are usually the larger ones. They appear within three days to a week after ice out on the main lake.

A very common misconception held by some anglers is that crappies are coming in right after ice out to spawn. Generally, the temperatures in shallow areas at the end of ice out which attracts crappies is approximately 52 degrees F, whereas spawning temperature is between 64° F and 68° F.

Ice out shallow water movement is not entirely unrelated to spawning. When the crappies move in they go on a merciless feeding frenzy. Fat taken in as a result of their eating binge is probably used in the development of eggs in the females. Crappies appear to need a lot of energy because they do not deliberately fast during spawning like some fish. There is no doubt that the males need every calorie they can obtain as they have few opportunities to eat once they establish a nest.

CANALS

As soon as you observe the last of the ice going out on a lake, head for any boat canal which might be connected to it.

As the water reaches the low 50's you will tire your arm out catching crappies. Try to locate those areas in the canal which are about 2½ to 4 feet deep with a dark muddy bottom. If there happens to be a few dead trees, limbs, or brush in the canal, that's the place to concentrate your efforts. You should check the canal daily until you begin to catch crappies. There is just such a series of canals on a major lake chain near my home. Each spring hundreds of crappies are taken there by anglers. By far, most of them are caught on jigs or minnows.

CATTAIL BAYS

Shallow, muddy, cattail-infested bottoms are outstanding crappie magnets just after ice out.

If the lakes in your area don't have canals, most of them will usually have a shallow marsh which has cattails. Cattails usually grow on very soft, muddy, dark bottoms and will draw crappies for the same reasons as canals. These areas are shallow enough to fish while wearing waders, but can be extremely dangerous. You will easily sink in the soft muck and may not be able to free yourself. Unless you can find a cattail area to fish from shore, I recommend that you use a boat and forget about wading.

SMALLER CONNECTING PONDS

Many larger lakes have smaller satellite ponds which are connected by streams, flooded lowlands, or sloughs. These satellite ponds heat up rapidly and can reach 70° F, while the main lake is still in the low 50's. These warm ponds will be filled with crappies escaping the colder water of the main lake. The perimeter of these ponds will be even warmer than their centers. You should first fish the entire perimeter of the pond. You will soon find that those areas which have downed trees are the most productive, although it's hard to go wrong anywhere in these ponds.

HOW TO FISH SHALLOW ICE OUT CRAPPIES

One way to fish crappies in cold shallow canals, cattail bays, or small ponds is to place a minnow or jig about 12 to 15 inches below a bobber and cast out as far as possible. If you see dead brush, limbs, or fallen trees in the water try to target these areas. Retrieve very slowly, turning your reel handle only one turn, then waiting for a second. Repeat this again and again until your lure or bait is right up against the bank or your boat. Often, shallow crappies will follow the intended meal and snatch it just as you are about to lift it from the water. This type of retrieve is deadly on crappies.

A bobber is an excellent way to fish cold shallow water crappies. It allows the bait or lure to be fished slowly without sinking and hanging up on the bottom.

I prefer to fish shallows without a bobber on the ultralight spinning gear recommended earlier. I tie on a marabou jig, hold the rod tip high, and slowly twitch the lure in. Nonetheless on some colder spring days, crappies will hit only the slowest-moving lures. Because the water you're fishing is so shallow, it becomes necessary on those slow days to add a bobber. This allows slow movement while preventing the lure from sinking and hanging up on the bottom.

FEEDER CREEKS AND CULVERTS

Amazingly productive places for catching crappies, even while the ice is still melting on lakes, are feeder creeks or streams and areas where culverts carry water from one lake to another. The movement of the water through culverts and the warmer temperatures that result from streams gathering solar heat as they flow across the land, attract various organisms which make up part of the crappies' food chain. These organisms flourish here, just as they will in the warming canals and cattail marshes.

But if these areas are shallow, (5 feet or less deep) these structures have to be fished almost exclusively at night, until the entire lake has thawed. If culverts or streams empty into much deeper water, fishing can be excellent even during the day. Winter's ice will disappear first wherever moving water enters a lake or river. As the ice retreats from shore and the shallows warm up, crappies are tempted to approach the shoreline. But they shyly hang back just under the edge of the ice. Crappies prefer to hide in low light under the ice, where

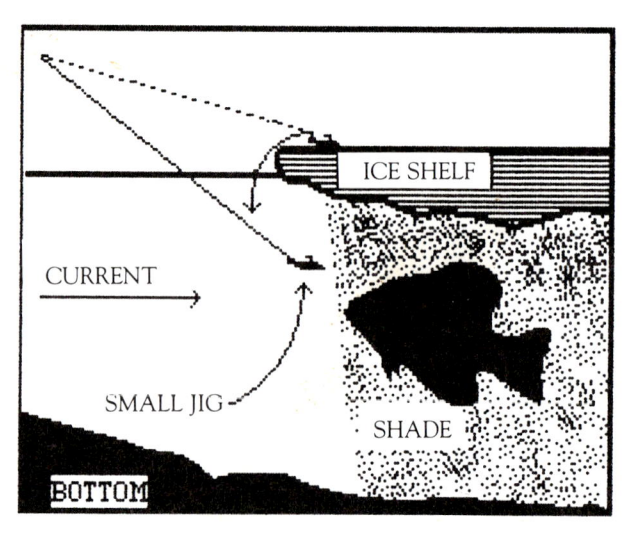

To catch crappies which hide in the shade of receding ice, cast a small panfish fly or 1/64th oz. jig onto the ice shelf and slowly slide it off the edge. Crappies will take it as it plummets.

the water is shaded from the sun. They will venture into the open water to approach a creek or culvert only under the protection of darkness.

When crappies are hiding just under the edge of the receding ice, they can easily be caught by casting a small panfish fly or 1/64th ounce jig onto the top of the ice next to the edge. Very carefully, raise your rod tip without reeling in your lure. As the rod tip rises, the lure will slip over the edge of the ice and flutter down in sight of the waiting fish. If you detect any movement of your line at all, set the hook.

Crappies have a definite preference for low light. This preference has a major influence on the daily behavior of a crappie.

A crappie will make every effort to stay in dark or shaded areas. If ample cover is not available, crappies will use the water's depth to escape the sun's penetration of the water. Because of their preference for low light conditions, most of them feed mainly during the darker hours of the day and rest during the brightest. Although a certain percentage of any given population of crappies will be alert throughout the day and can be caught, the best hours to fish for crappies are around sunset and sunrise.

If you find a feeder creek or culvert which spills into a good crappie lake and there is still some ice on the lake, you should give night fishing a try, using a lighted bobber and a minnow. Although I usually avoid using minnows, there is no better way to fish under night conditions.

My personal avoidance of using minnows partly stems from convenience and partly from compassion. In most situations minnows really aren't necessary. Consider the time you'll save not having to constantly bait your hook and the money you save not having to buy minnows every time you fish. Besides, no one wishes to be needlessly wasteful of life, however lowly the creature. (Although, I agree mosquitoes can push their luck in a hurry.) Since I've come to appreciate the effectiveness of marabou jigs, I rarely use minnows except in the winter and at night.

Since crappies are mainly sight feeders, jigs do not work as well at night. The most successful night rig that I've seen has a minnow hooked about three feet below a lighted bobber. The minnow is hooked on a number #6 hook just above its excrement vent. This area of the minnow is very fleshy and contains no vital organs. You will neither kill nor incapacitate it.

It's important to keep the minnow alive since the crappie will be relying considerably on its vibration-sensitive lateral line to detect the presence of the minnow's movement. Dead minnows don't move. Neither do those that have been impaled through the back for very long. A minnow will stay alive and move about considerably more if hooked as illustrated.

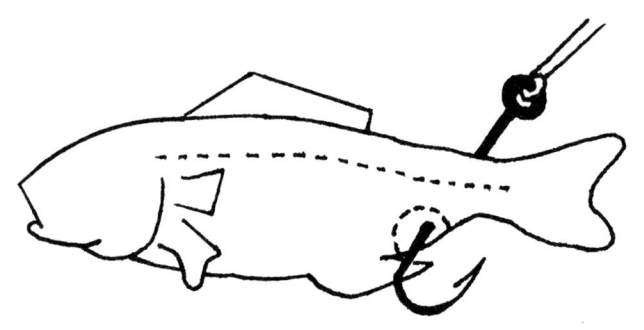

Hooked in this manner with a number six hook, a minnow will swim about more freely, live longer, and therefore be more productive.

Day or night the best way to fish flowing water from feeder creeks or culverts is to cast a minnow or jig just off the edge of the moving water where it seems to stop its flow as it mixes with the surrounding water. The crappies will be stacked up in the calm water just on the edge of the churning current waiting to ambush smaller prey which are attracted to the flow or washed into the receiving waters by the current.

When you cast your jig or minnow into these areas, very slowly reel in. It's not a good idea to work a jig or bait with fast jerks especially in moving water. About the time a crappie is going to eat the thing, you'll snatch it away from him. You don't have to worry about making your presentation seem lifelike in moving water. A properly hooked minnow will create all the action it needs on its own. And the flow of the water will animate the feathers if you use a marabou jig. The crappie will do the rest.

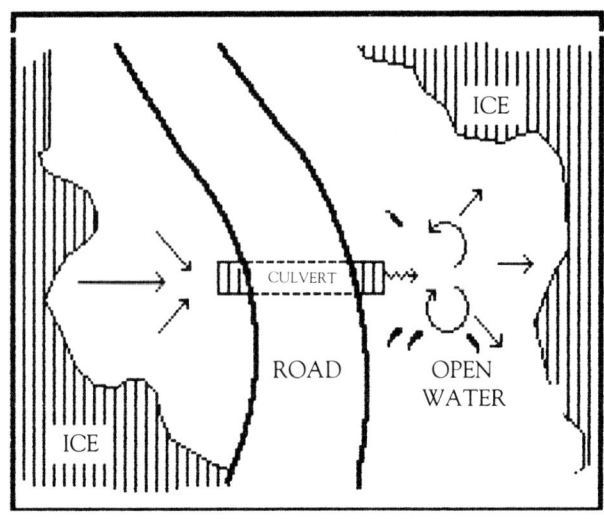

As temperatures rise and more crappies begin to seek the warm shallows, culverts and streams become even more productive. Crappies can be taken even in the daytime, once the general area of water around these flows reaches the 50's. In fact, some culverts and streams will continue to produce fish throughout spring and summer if there is deep water nearby.

When ice first begins to melt, look for crappies at night in the calmer water alongside the churning, turbulent currents created as water flows through culverts (above) or enters from a feeder creek or stream (below). When the ice has melted completely, these structures will hold crappies during the day.

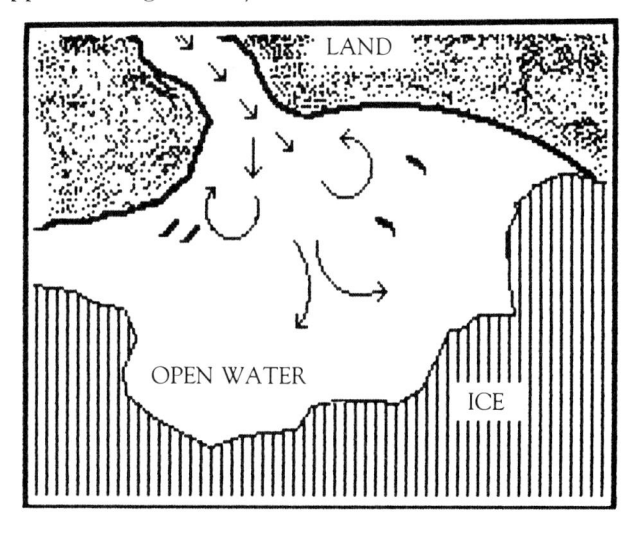

Under Cover Crappies and Other Shallow Shady Secrets

POKE FISHING FLOATING CATTAILS

An excellent but virtually unknown location for fishing crappies is within the shadows beneath floating mobile cattail bogs or "mobiles." Floating cattail mobiles are formed when rising water levels dislodge large sections of cattails from the soft muddy bottoms they're usually rooted in. These sections are made up of thousands of connected buoyant roots and other organic matter, including the long, leafy stemmed plant itself. In fact, they are so buoyant that duck hunters have long used them as floating blinds. Sometimes entire cattail marshes are uprooted and pushed by the wind to various locations around the lake where they come to rest against new shorelines. They can be quite a nuisance blocking boat canals, drifting onto beaches, and plugging culverts.

Whatever problems cattails might present to people, crappies love them, and so do northern pike and bass. They are in effect, giant shade umbrellas. In the spring before new stem growth begins, the great bulk of organic mass of the cattail mobiles becomes a solar collector. The stored heat is conducted into the water below, giving crappies the early spring warmth they seek. The crappie has the best of worlds because he can stay there warm and shaded.

Crappies will seek the cover of cattail mobiles even in the summer as shallow lake water temperatures rise to uncomfortable highs. During the summer the tips of the new growth of vegetation intercepts the sun's heat, preventing the floating organic mass below from becoming too hot. In deep lakes, crappies can swim deep enough to find cool water and low light conditions. However, in lakes that are shallow, crappies have a difficult time escaping the deadly harsh summer sun and heat. The floating mats become life-savers for the crappies.

Summer cattail stems perform the same function as the radials on an air conditioner that conduct heat away from the unit. Heat radiates up the stems of cattails and is given off to the surrounding air, actually cooling the mass and the water beneath the structure. This cooler shaded water gives the crappie a place to escape from the lethal temperatures of open shallow water.

Some mobiles are better crappie structure than others. Those mobiles which push up against a sloping shoreline near deep water will hold more crappies. The lake side of the mobile will remain afloat and give crappies as well as other game fish an excellent place to hide.

THE BEST METHODS FOR FISHING CATTAIL MOBILES

Unless you have some type of watercraft or a wading tube you will be unable to effectively fish cattail mobiles. They have to be approached from the water's deepest side. Slowly move your craft right alongside the structure and "poke fish" the hollowed-out shaded spaces or clearings beneath the bottom of the floating cattails.

As you ease along the edge of these floating crappie hotels you will find that the root system or the water depth in some spots will not allow room for crappies to hide beneath them. Look for areas which form an overhanging shelf with a clearing below. Wearing polarized sunglasses while fishing cattail mobiles is crucial. Unless you use polarized lenses you won't be able to see beneath the water's surface to locate these shaded clearings.

Once you find these shelves, you will often find hundreds of minnows swimming along the edge. The presence of minnows is a sure sign that crappies are probably just beneath the shelf in the darkness. They lie in wait for a careless minnow to drop down too low. If crappies aren't present, these minnows will themselves seek the comfort of darkness beneath and you may not see them.

Polarized sunglasses allow the angler to see into the water, revealing those spaces where crappies can easily swim beneath the cattails. Note the minnows along the edge of the shelf.

Except for the lure itself, this is one place that fancy fishing gear means very little. You can use your marabou jig with about any pound test line and even use a broom handle for a fishing rod if you prefer. But two different types of poles are recommended for this type of situation: a short 28 to 30-inch winter fishing jig stick and a very long pole or rod over 10 feet in length for "jigger-poling." Tie a jig about 3 or 4 feet below the tip of the tiny rod and 6 feet from the tip of the jigger-pole; no reel is needed.

With the short pole, slowly lower or "poke" the jig into the clearing below the overhang and be prepared to set the hook immediately. If the lure is placed in sight of a crappie, he will grab it so fast you'll hardly have time to react if you're not prepared. If you don't get one right away, slowly yo-yo (vertically jig) the lure up and down several times before moving to the next clearing. The crappie might be looking off in another direction and his lateral line will alert him to the jig's movement as it's raised and lowered.

Cattails grow in huge clumps and their edges are quite irregular. Moving along them, you will find numerous open spaces or indentations in the cattails. As long as you are fishing along the straightaway, the short winter fishing pole is the best choice. The longer pole is used to reach back into the gaps in the vegetation where your craft can't go. Not only is there an abundance of hungry crappies under cattail mobiles, but generally they are larger than average. After all, this is prime real estate and the biggest fish take the best places.

UNDER COVER CRAPPIES AND OTHER
SHALLOW SHADY SECRETS

Lower a jig into the shaded clearances below floating cattails to catch lunker crappies. Visored caps and polarized sunglasses worn by these young anglers allow them to locate the clearings beneath the water's surface glare.

WATER HYACINTHS

In the gulf states and especially in Florida, jigger-poling, ("poke fishing") is quite effective along the edges of water hyacinths from mid February through late autumn. Water hyacinths are not rooted to the bottom, and like floating cattails, offer excellent cover for crappies. Hyacinths which are found in streams, small rivers, and feeder creeks are the most productive in late spring through summer. In lakes they shelter fish spring, summer, and fall.

You fish them almost exactly the same way you do cattail mobiles except you use regular spinning gear and jigger-poles instead of the winter jiggle stick. Since hyacinths do not grow to the heights of cattails, the angler can maneuver a spinning rod more easily there than in and among tall cattails. Be careful as you ease along floating mats of water hyacinths. Poisonous water snakes and alligators can put undesired excitement into your fishing trip.

Floating water hyacinths in streams, rivers, and feeder creeks are excellent crappie collectors and can be fished by jigging or poking lures slowly around the edges.

FISHING PIERS, BOAT DOCKS, SWIMMING PLATFORMS

Remember the man in chapter one who was confronted for having 754 crappies in possession? He was angling from a fishing pier. That pier is located near an area of the lake which drops off dramatically to deeper water. In the spring, these structures offer the warmth of shallow water and low light conditions for crappies. Being close to the safety of deep water makes them especially appealing to fish. It gives boatless anglers access to fish.

When fishing these piers, you simply work your lure along the pier itself. The fish will be hiding in the shade. You work fishing docks and swimming platforms the same way. During summer months these areas are not as productive except at night. In the southern states, piers and boat docks often have manmade fish attracters within casting distance of the platforms. These are usually brush piles or even discarded Christmas trees weighted down by stones.

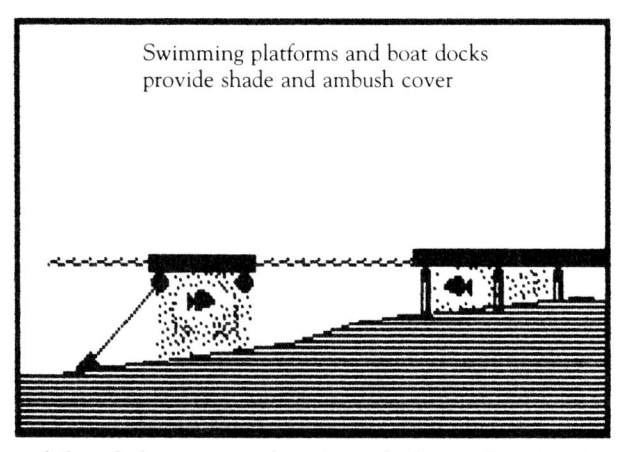

Crappies seek low light areas under piers, docks, and swimming platforms.

BRIDGES

In Minneapolis, Minnesota, there is a very long bridge which spans the entrance of a small bay on the west side of Cedar Lake. Cedar Lake is noted as much for its jogging paths, as for its excellent crappie fishing. In spring as crappies begin to crowd the warm bay and seek the shade of the bridge, scores of anglers line the overpass to intercept the incoming fish.

Near the bridge is a parking lot and a few side streets where anglers also park. On more than one occasion, the stretch between that bridge and nearby parked cars became jogging paths for me, as I've had to chase anglers trying to make a break for their cars with huge pails of too many fish!

On one such occasion, a rather elderly gentleman spotted me just as I began checking licenses on the far end of the bridge about 100 yards away. As I look at licenses I always watch out of the corner of my eye to see if someone acts suspiciously or attempts to leave the bridge in a hurry. This elderly gentleman did just that. Leaving his wife and fishing equipment, no doubt to pick up later, he grabbed his pail of crappies and dashed for his car.

Because of his age and the very large number of fish he was carrying, he didn't quite make it to his auto before I caught up to him. We were both embarrassed by the situation as he explained that he didn't really need the fish and that he had never done anything like this before. Since he didn't need the fish, I asked him why he had risked falling down and breaking a hip trying to run away with the crappies. To my further embarrassment, he told me that he compared his age to my weight and figured he could outrun me! He almost did.

The best way to fish bridges is to cast your lure or bait underneath, back into the shaded areas where the crappies hide, and slowly retrieve your lure, or else just lower the lure alongside the shade and yo-yo it up and down to entice the crappies to come after it. If you can't cast underneath a bridge, attach a bobber to your line and lower the rig on the upwind side of the bridge. The wind will take your presentation to the fish. Try to fish as closely to the pilings or supports as you can.

Lighted bridges are outstanding locations for night fishing. The lights draw insect which fall into the water. Hungry baitfish and crappies are drawn to such areas. Please remember never to fish from bridges without walkways, especially at night.

Spring crappies love bridges. And no matter what part of the country you live in you can find them under those bridges which cross areas where larger lakes or rivers connect to small ponds or bays.

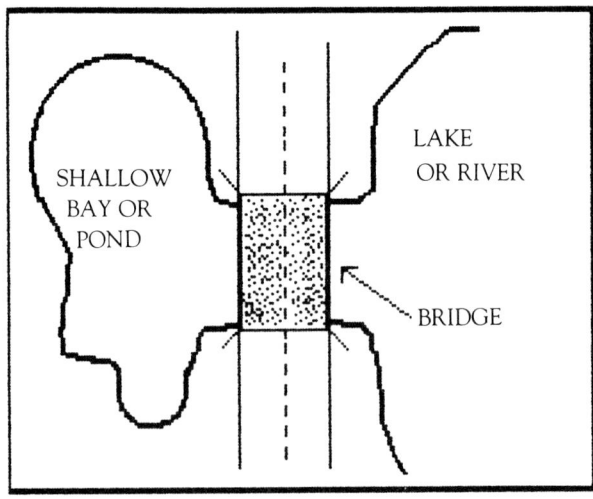

Crappies seek the shade of bridges where narrows connect large bodies of water to small ponds or bays.

BULRUSHES OR "REEDS"

Bulrushes are hollow-stemmed emergent plants that look like long, green, pointed pencils. Depending on the variety some will grow six or seven feet above the water; others only a foot. They are usually found in shallow water growing on hard sandy bottoms. In northern states during the winter, the green stem of the plant dies but remains intact. Crappies are attracted to rushes, commonly called reeds by many anglers. Rushes have three distinctly separate crappie-producing patterns: ice out, spawn, and summer darkness.

ICE OUT

In northern states the long, hard winter of snow and ice has erased less hardy species of plants, but rushes are so durable that the stems from the previous season of these emergent plants can still be seen sticking above the water after spring ice out. Although their visible stems are lifeless after the winter die-back of submerged aquatic vegetation, rushes are often the only protective cover available for crappies and creatures they prey upon in the warming spring shallows.

For ice out rushes to be productive, they must be located near deep water. Crappies will bite mainly during low light hours in this pattern. They'll move into the rushes during the evening and you can clean up on them for about two hours; they'll return again at sunup. Because reeds are often the only cover in the spring, you can expect them to contain several species of fish. Rock bass, jumbo perch, walleyes, and northern pike all seek the cover of ice out reeds.

The best bulrush communities are those which protrude from shore on sandy points. The points sticking out from shore serve as a guide fence and corral for fish that might otherwise swim aimlessly in search for shallow structure. When you fish ice out rushes, always work the point and edges first to intercept those crappies which can easily retreat to the safety of deeper water. Then slowly work your way toward the center of the plant community. This pattern will only last for about

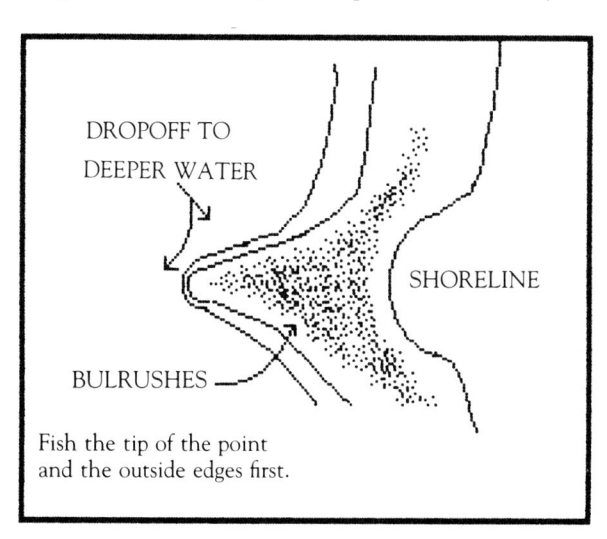

DROPOFF TO DEEPER WATER

SHORELINE

BULRUSHES

Fish the tip of the point and the outside edges first.

Rushes on sandy points will hold fish shortly after ice out. Fishing the point and edges first will prevent the retreat of crappies to deeper water.

two weeks, while water temperatures range from 42 F. to 50 F. Then crappies will move back to deeper water until spawning time.

Ice out rushes near deep water are often the only protective spring cover for crappies and their prey.

SPAWNING IN THE RUSHES

Any lake which has a good population of rushes will provide the angler with a crappie fishing bonanza during spawning season! When water temperatures in the bulrush communities approach 67° F, crappies crowd into reeds in great numbers to spawn. By this time, the fresh green growths of this year's crop of rushes are four to eight inches above the water's surface.

Because rushes grow on hard sandy bottoms, they become preferred spawning grounds second only to flooded timber. Hard surfaces are preferable because of the easy maintenance and stability of such a surface. Male crappies sweep out nests about one and a half times as wide as their body is long. They locate their nest in and around the base of the newly emerging stems of the "reeds." Fairly flat rocks or pieces of waterlogged wood scattered among the reeds are magnets to spawning crappies looking for maintenance-free areas to establish their nests.

One interesting spawning site that I observed in rushes was established on the back of a collapsed metal folding chair. Apparently the chair had fallen overboard from perhaps a pontoon or was abandoned on the ice and made its way to the bottom. An opportunistic male crappie had set up his nest over it without having to sweep the bottom. And he aggressively defended his little throne from all pretenders.

FISHING RUSHES

As water temperatures reach the upper 60's it's time again to put on your polarized sunglasses. By push poling, drifting, sculling, rowing, or carefully easing through the rushes with an electric trolling motor, you will have no problem locating crappies on their nests. Gently lower a jig or minnow in front and slightly above the fish with a long fishing rod or a jigger-pole and hang on. Although your rod is hanging over the fish, it won't spook them because it looks like another reed.

Without polarized glasses, it's still possible to find crappies by random casting. But reeds are nearly impossible to cast and retrieve jigs in. You will angrily experience constant snags on the stems unless you are spot fishing only the openings where the reeds grow rather sparsely. You can prevent much of the stem snagging by barely moving your jig through the forest of stems extremely slowly; the lure will bounce around the rushes better. The stems are so tough, that once you have snagged one, it's nearly impossible to pull your hook free with the recommended 4 pound test line. If you are using the cast and retrieve method, try to fish only open pockets in the rushes and you'll save yourself a lot of misery.

If you find only males on the nests, you can usually find the larger females in deeper water near the spawning area waiting for the cover of darkness to approach the nests. However, during the peak of spawning, both can be seen on a nest together. A female crappie can get much bigger than males, but most of the time spawning crappies are fairly well-matched in size.

Any time an angler is fishing bulrushes, he should take extreme care to do as little damage to these plants as possible. These plants are living filters which help maintain a healthy aquatic environment by breaking down pollutants. They are an environmental treasure that must be protected.

Spawning female and male crappies caught in bulrushes; females usually grow bigger. Notice the lack of black beneath the gills of the female contrasted with the male's full spawning coloration.

SUMMER DARKNESS

Post spawn crappies will usually only return to reeds at night or on very dark cloudy days. And then only to those rushes with deep water nearby. Because of the presence of giant bass and northern pike in summer rushes, crappies won't penetrate the reeds as they do after ice out or during spawning unless there is pondweed present. Pondweed fishing is a distinct pattern in itself and will be discussed presently. Summer night fishing around rushes is best accomplished by still fishing a minnow below a lighted bobber along the edge of the rushes.

The easiest way to fish rushes, especially after dark, is with a long pole. A lure or natural bait can be lowered to the fish without hanging up on the tough stems of the reeds.

Whenever you fish in bulrushes, fishing requires a lot of patience. You're going to hang your lure up often no matter how hard you try and you will lose a few. As with almost all excellent crappie structures, those reeds which are near deep water are the best. If you work at it and try fishing them shortly after ice out, during the spawning season, or at night you should catch crappies.

They're in the Trees!

These beautiful spawning giant males were caught in flooded timber on black and pink/yellow marabou jigs.

FLOODED TIMBER

There may be no structure more associated with crappie fishing than flooded timber. Since trees seemingly aren't natural to a crappie's environment, it's quite fascinating that they actually prefer timber over other physical structures. The explanation is simple. Timber accommodates crappies with permanent ambush cover, attracts aquatic creatures they prey upon, provides temperature and low light comfort, and offers a hard, stable surface for spawning. With minor exceptions there are three basic types of flooded timber which are the most productive: fallen trees, cypress tree roots, and beaver lodges which are mixtures of mud and timber.

FALLEN TREES AND BRUSH

Throughout the United States great reservoirs of water to supply power plants, have been created in the process of building dams. In this process, thousands of forested acres have been deliberately flooded. As nature took its course, the flooded trees eventually died and within a few years wind and water erosion began to topple them. In the easier-to-reach areas where some of the more valuable timber was removed prior to flooding, great stump fields, trimmed limbs, and brush were left behind. The resulting eerie-looking underwater landscape became home to an explosion of aquatic populations.

The larger the trunk of the fallen tree the better it will be for attracting crappies.

Crappies are attracted to toppled flooded trees because of the cover and forage they provide. A dead tree which has tumbled into the water will create more shade and offer more hiding spaces for bait fish than it did when it was upright. And the larger the fallen tree, the better it will be for attracting crappies. They will also seek out the discarded limbs and brush piles left over from logging for the same reasons. The leftover stump fields are pretty much used only for spawning platforms, although they might be used for cover if they have extensive and exposed roots. The world records for both white and black crappies came from such reservoirs.

The creation of flooded timber is not always done on so grand a scale as that of impounding reservoirs. By stark contrast it might be no more than the dropping of a single tree into the water by a beaver. The dramatic action of high winds or the slow subtle erosion of a shoreline will put trees in the water, creating excellent crappie structure. Timber is flooded naturally by the seasonal torrential rise of rivers and creeks from melting snow and spring rains and the rhythm of lake-level fluctuations which take place over decades. A lake which has been slowly drying up may eventually claim back large areas of the surrounding shore where trees have taken root and matured during the water's absence.

The massive trunks and maze of limbs of toppled dead trees create the same low-light conditions that crappies seek under docks, piers, and floating cattail mats. Additionally, trees readily absorb the rays of the sun in the spring storing heat which they radiate back to the surrounding water. If a winter-wearied crappie wants to warm up, it simply hugs up to a sun-soaked tree.

Late one March day, I was fishing timber in the Santee-Cooper Reservoir in South Carolina. I had searched in vain all day for crappies without a hit. I watched other anglers and no one was taking fish. The water temperatures were averaging 59° F. A severe cold front was moving through the area, but I knew that there had to be hungry fish somewhere.

In this part of the state the reservoir water is quite turbid. It's nearly impossible to see what your lure is doing below the water. Snags and lost lures were my story for the day. Trying not to lose too many jigs, I had been rather cautious about jigging too close to the flooded trees. It turns out that is the opposite of what I should have been doing.

After making a cast that can best be described as squirrel fishing, I had to ease my boat up to the tree to free my lure from the limbs which were sticking out of the water. As I grabbed the limb to keep my balance I felt the limb's warmth which was stored from the day's sun. If I could feel it, I wondered if the crappies could. I decided to lower the jig down right alongside the trunk of the tree, practically crawling the lure down the bark. To my delight I felt a familiar tap and I set the hook. I had hooked a two pound black crappie. Using this approach I continued to catch fish and ended the day with a beautiful "mess" of one to two pound fish.

Shortly after ice out when water temperatures are below 55 F. crappies will seek timber in extremely shallow water (three feet or less). From 55 F. up to spawning temperatures, which is usually close to 67 F., crappies seek timber at any depth just as long as some of the timber is near enough to the surface of the water to absorb the sun's penetrating rays.

Later for spawning purposes crappies will seek level and near level spawning platforms on the timber in about three to five feet of water. While crappies spawn fairly close to the surface of the water, the platform they're on might reach down into 15 feet of water. The crucial thing to a spawning crappie is the depth of the platform they spawn on, not the depth of the water. Generally, anglers will see crappies spawning on the bottom in just a few feet of water. But they are not there because it's the bottom. They're there because the bottom in that particular location happens to be close to the surface. In other words, any stable object close to the top of the water will serve as a spawning platform.

Those platforms which are elevated up to within a few feet of the water's surface from deeper water and are relatively wide are a crappie's first choice for spawning.*

Fallen flooded trees fit this category perfectly. And from a male crappie's point of view there's a very sensible reason for this. Male crappies prefer to select spawning platforms near deep water where females congregate in preparation for spawning. Nests which are near deep water are the first to intercept the incoming females. Since the females won't have to risk travel into the hazardous shallows, they, too, prefer the elevated platforms. I have seen as many as four females together depositing their eggs on one male's timber nest near deep water.

Even if timber is not over deeper water, crappies still prefer it to the bottom of the lake. After all, a nice tree trunk doesn't have to be cleaned or swept out to prepare a suitable nest as would the debris-covered lake bottom. So trees or very wide limbs are selected even when they are lying right on the bottom. If the timber is too small to form a platform for the crappie but is at the right depth and near a hard surfaced bottom, then crappies will make their nests just alongside the timber. If you suspect crappies are spawning in a body of water you intend to fish, you should first head for the timber. You can easily find the males on patrol carefully guarding their nests on stumps, trunks, wide limbs, or cleanly swept sand craters next to narrow timber or brush.

When fishing downed timber or dead brush try casting to the less obstructed trunk or stump end first. During spawning season you will be able to see crappies at these locations through polarized sunglasses. Make sure you work your lure along both sides of the tree trunk, allowing the lure to drop below the level of the tree into the shadows. During spawning larger females are often in the shadows of the toppled trunk.

You may actually see the crappie engulf your lure as it rises for it. Don't wait for a tap on the line. Set the hook! Or, sometimes you may not even see a fish, but your lure has simply disappeared. Set the hook! Very often you will see a fish coming up for your lure but you see a strange white flash in the water right where your lure should be. Once again, set the hook! As a crappie flares his mouth to vacuum in your lure it reveals the white flesh inside its mouth. That can only mean it had its mouth open coming in your direction to swallow your lure or bait.

Next, you should work the open edges of the tree crown (branched area) by slowly lowering your lure through the topside of the limbs. As you thin out the outside crappies, you can ease your boat over the

*FOOTNOTE: It should be noted that white crappies will spawn in from only two inches of water to depths of five feet. Black crappies will spawn from 10 inches deep to six feet or more. However, the average spawning depth for both is about three to five feet.

ABOVE: A male crappie anxiously guards his timber nest. The trunk of the tree in this photo was five feet deep whereas the bottom of the lake at this location was eight feet deep. The crappie preferred the elevated platform. BELOW: If the timber is not wide enough but at the right depth, crappies will nest alongside it.

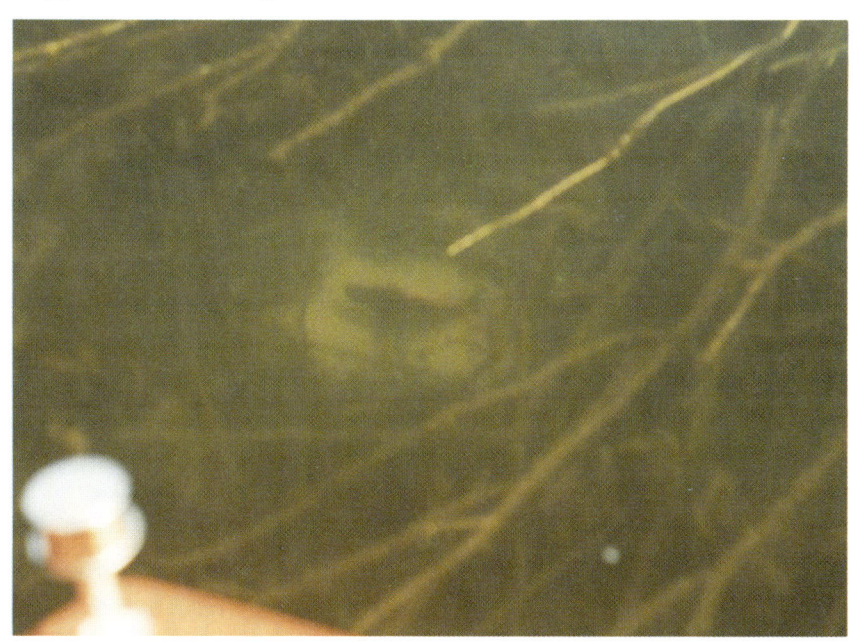

center of the tree and yo-yo your jig right down in the thicker branches. Because of the number of the branches in a tree top, a crappie is not as likely to be distracted by heavy line in this situation. To fish tree tops some anglers use 30 pound test line which most assuredly looks like a branch itself. If they do hang up, they simply horse the lure free or break off the limb. I have found this method quite effective in extremely thick tree tops or brush. You will lose some lures, however. And if you are fishing timber properly, you have to expect this.

These crappie anglers (boat on left) would be much more successful if they were fishing right in the flooded timber of this eastern lake.

Generally, most flooded timber areas involve large numbers of trees so you should remember to search for the largest toppled or leaning trees you can find near deep water. Occasionally, you will find a lake that might hold only one or two downed trees. Make sure you check them out. Among the many beautiful lakes of Wisconsin, there is one particular lake within an hour's drive from my home which has brought me many hours of fishing enjoyment. It has no timber structure except for one toppled dead tree trunk about 40 feet from shore. In that entire lake there is no spot which produces crappies as well as by that tree. You'll catch five or six fish around it, wait 30 minutes, then catch a few more which have moved in.

Sometimes a lake might be filled with timber, but only the isolated trees will hold fish. Such was the case one mid April in South Carolina's Santee-Cooper. I had been catching only small fish in the feeder creeks and decided to search the acres of flooded dead timber, in an area known as Jack's Creek. I wasn't alone. Scores of boats were slowly electro-trolling through the timber vertically jigging around every tree. I tried my luck as well. After a couple hours of hard fishing, I had taken only one really nice fish. Those that hadn't already been thinned out must have been spooked by all the activity.

Search for the largest toppled or leaning trees you can find near deep water. Those that stick off to themselves are often the best.

Off at a distance I noticed a very large isolated tree trunk barely sticking from the water at an angle. I motored over to it. The tree trunk was about two and one half feet wide; the crown of the tree was missing. I positioned the boat at one end of the log and cast to the other. As soon as the little jig sank beneath the log an unmistakable twitch in my line told me somebody was home. After setting the hook, I thought the log had come alive and was swimming off with my fishing gear! Without the benefit of a scale in my boat I estimated that the crappie approached two pounds. I then motored to a number of such isolated trees and caught several more nice crappies in the same weight range. Because these trees weren't in with the mass of timber, they had been overlooked by all the other anglers. And I sure didn't mind.

CYPRESS TREE ROOTS

In the rivers, creeks, and lakes of Florida and the southern most parts of other gulf states, crappies are found in very shallow timber from the late winter through the end of summer. And, most notably, around the roots of cypress trees. This conifer grows from Texas to Delaware along coastal swamps and can easily grow in water. It also thrives inland throughout many low, swampy areas of the south and is found as far north as Illinois.

This unusual tree has a special appeal to crappies (and largemouth bass) because of its root system. Weird tentacle-looking roots part and spread out before entering the soil beneath the water to give support to the tree. These roots form a labyrinth of low light hiding places preferred by crappies.

Some cypress roots grow sideways and form knobby structures on them commonly called "knees." These knees protrude through the surface of the water around the tree. The presence of knees around a cypress alerts the angler to beware of the lateral roots which hold them. You will have to fish cypress trees which have knees with a very long jigger-pole. Whether you're fishing from shore or a boat the jigger-pole allows you to reach and "poke" in and around the tree's roots rather than cast to it. Casting to a kneed cypress will usually result in numerous frustrating snags while you try to work your lure slowly through the maze of roots. Cypress roots makes excellent spawning platforms when they are two to four feet beneath the water's surface.

They're in the Trees!

Note the tentacle-looking roots of these cypress trees exposed by low river water conditions. During a season of normal water levels, over 30 crappies each weighing nearly 2 pounds were caught and released by the author from these roots within a 25-yard stretch of this very shoreline.

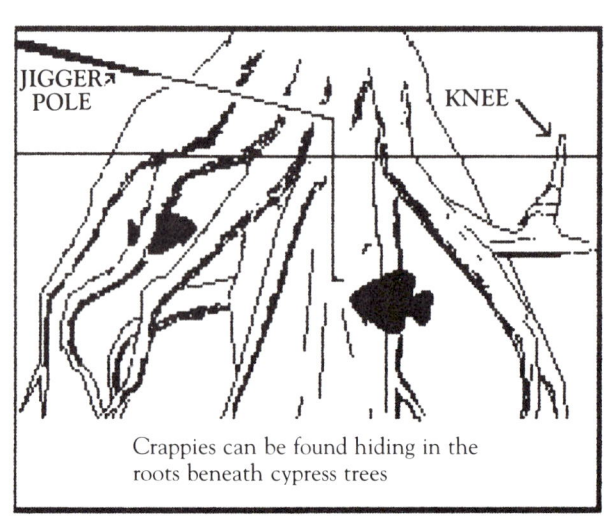

Crappies can be found hiding in the roots beneath cypress trees

Casting lures into the roots of a cypress tree will result in snags. The best way to fish them is by jigging a marabou lure in and around the maze of roots where the crappies hide.

The author jigger-poles a 1 pound crappie from the cypress roots on Newnan's Lake located near Gainesville, Fla. Newnan's Lake has the honor of yielding Florida's 3 lbs. 12 oz. state record crappie (speckled perch).

BEAVER LODGES

During the spring the right type of beaver lodges will outproduce all other types of timber structure. Not only will the crappies pile up there immediately after ice out, but they will stay there right through spawning. It's possible to take crappies from beaver lodges for a month and a half straight.

Beaver lodges, of course, are the hollow-domed wooden and mud "houses" constructed by the furry little engineer as its home. The dome always sticks above the water line and is an efficient solar heat collector. There are two conditions that must be met for beaver lodges to pay off. First, they must be constructed near deep water, and second, they must be made of very dark mud and wood.

A beaver lodge in a bay or small pond which connects to a larger body of crappie-populated water is a fantastic crappie structure if located near deep water.

The deep water requirement is fairly constant in most crappie structure arrangements since this anxious fish likes to stay fairly close to the darkness and safety of deeper water. The abundance of brush and wood in the lodge attracts baitfish and aquatic insects. No self-respecting crappie will overlook the feeding opportunities around a beaver house. In fact, walleyes and largemouth bass are also attracted to these domed dinner tables.

Crappies are also attracted to the lodges for the comfort and convenience afforded by the warmth of the dome. Because the top of the beaver house sticks out of the water three or four feet, it easily soaks up the heat of the sun. The great mass of mud with which the beaver constructs and plasters his house is capable of storing a tremendous amount of solar heat.

Because the base of the lodge is under the water line much of the heat which is absorbed is radiated directly back into the surrounding water. Ice out crappies cannot resist these solar heaters. Spring water temperatures can average 15 degrees warmer immediately next to a lodge than throughout the rest of the lake. And the gently sloping sides of the structure just beneath the water makes excellent spawning platforms. Once you have found a lodge, move your boat slowly up to it and very often you can see the crappies swimming about in the maze of sticks and brush around its base.

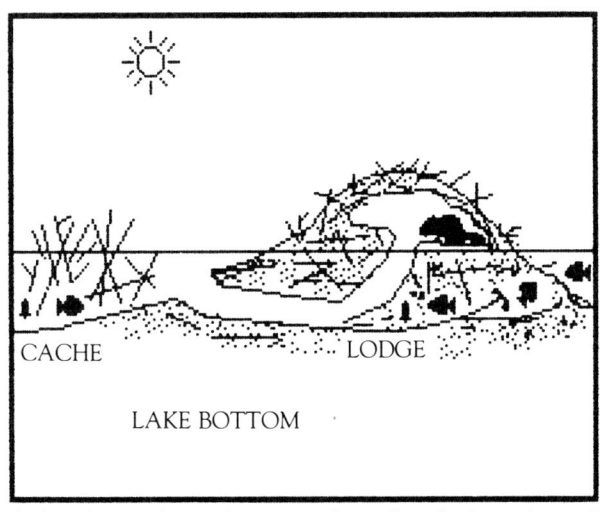

The beaver lodge dome above the water line absorbs heat from the sun and conducts it to the surrounding water. Ice out and spawn-ready crappies seek the warmth of the lodge.

Before winter sets in and the lakes freeze over, beaver will create a large cache of food beneath the water near their lodge. They chew off small branches from toppled trees then stick these in the mud for easy winter access. As spring rolls around, quite often much of the debris from the cache remain; if the beaver have been trapped out, almost all of the cache might remain. Crappies love these caches. And this is the area around a lodge that you should fish first.

Approach the lodge wearing polarized sunglasses. You should be able to see hidden beneath the water scores of sticks and pieces of brush stuck in the mud surrounding the beaver house; this will likely be the cache. Start casting your jig toward the lodge beyond the edges of the cache and slowly retrieve your lure back through the tops of the sticks and twigs. Make a complete circle of the house, fishing only the cache area first.

After you have fished the cache in a complete circle of the lodge, you can then tighten the circle and fish right up to the lodge. This is when the proverbial patience of a fishermen is helpful because this is the place you may lose your first lures of the season and test you casting and retrieving skills. The faint of heart should put on a bobber to keep the lure above the stickups and slowly work his lure over the maze of sticks.

If you are bravely going bobberless and do hang up on the timber, simply move as close to the stick as possible, reel your line all the way in so that your rod tip is touching the offending snag, and push. Your lure should come loose. Most of the time a crappie will probably have your lure before it snags.

FREEING YOUR LURE FROM TIMBER

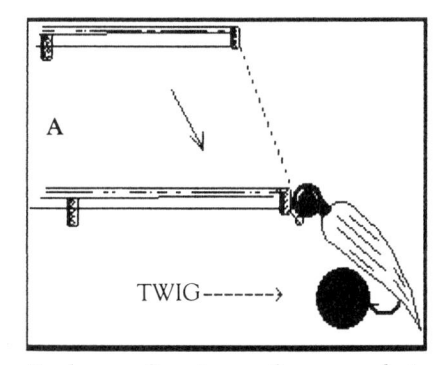

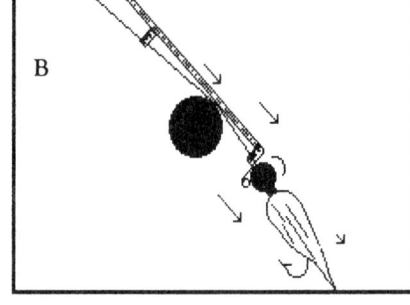

Reel your line in until your rod tip pushes up against the lure.

PUSH your rod tip and lure away from the snag.

If the wind is overwhelming the control of your boat around the lodge, you should approach it from the downwind side. Once you have fished out the downwind side, bring your boat right up to the lodge and climb on top of the mound. You can then fish the entire area. You won't hurt the lodge but you can hurt yourself; after all, lodges are covered with slippery mud and sharp sticks. Please be careful. Under no circumstances should you climb onto one that has a nest of geese or other feathered friends on its top. Some will.

If you prefer to fish a beaver lodge by standing on it, you will find that a jigger-pole will work nicely here. In the immediate area of the lodge you won't have to cast. You can just lower your jig into the water and yo-yo it up and down around the sticks and brush. With polarized glasses you can actually see the crappies swimming around

They're in the Trees!

These newspaper-sized crappies were caught from alongside a beaver lodge in a small pond which connected to a large lake.

the lodge. Place the jig just in front and slightly above them. Chances are you won't even feel the strike. You will either see a flash of white or simply realize that the lure has disappeared. Set the hook by snapping your pole tip upward.

RESERVOIR CREEK CHANNELS

An excellent pattern for fishing reservoir timber that is still standing is along the edges of pre-flood creek channels. These can be located with the aid of contour maps or electronic depth finders. In fact, most are fairly easy to find just by looking for the edge of the old tree lines. This pattern is fished by vertically jigging those trees which are the nearest to the creek channel. Lower your lure right to the bottom of the tree and yo-yo it up and down to draw attention to it.

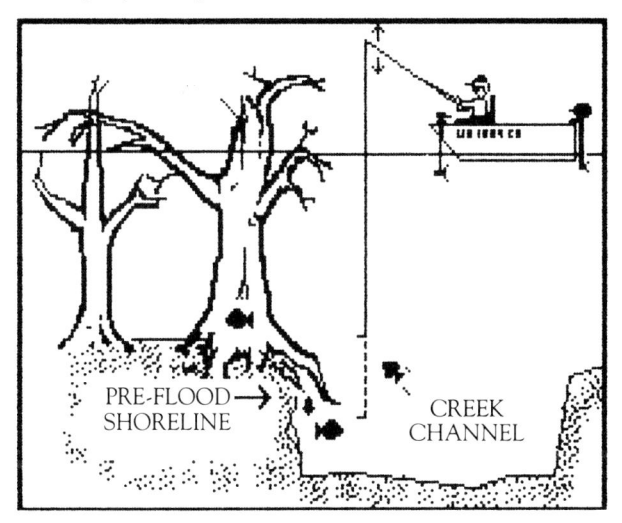

Winter or summer, deep water or shallow, the most important thing to remember about timber-fishing methods is this: When crappies are in timber they practically rub against the trees, roots, or lodges. You must get your lure as close to the structure as you possibly can. Take along extra jigs because if you are fishing timber properly you are going to lose lures. But, you sure will catch fish.

Cabbage Patch Fish and the Summer School Gang

Larger photo: Just prior to spawning and immediately afterward, this plant holds the secret to successful crappie fishing.

Smaller photo: Pondweed in its natural setting. Wearing polarized sunglasses will allow the angler to locate communities of pondweed where crappies can be hiding. Note the stalk-like spike ("candle") growing at the top of these early-to-mid summer plants.

PONDWEEDS *

After the little rascals are through spawning, crappies become hard to find. Aggressive male blue gills have moved in to spawn in many of the same areas which were used only a couple weeks earlier by their speckled cousins. Unable to find crappies, most avid panfishermen switch over to sunfish. Where do the crappies go after spawning? Are they still aggressive? Can they still be caught?

After spawning they are indeed aggressive, and will go on a feeding binge which lasts intensely for about two weeks. The males which have been riveted to their nesting areas for days will behave ravenously -- turning into eating machines. The females will also feed heavily, because their body cavities which were once filled with eggs are empty. They will waste no time filling back up with food and staying stuffed.

Furthermore, by the end of the spawning cycle, increasing water temperatures will raise the crappies' metabolic rate. (The rate of their food digestion will speed up.) This change in their metabolism forces them to consume more food to maintain normal energy levels.

Those which spawn next to deep timber may simply drop a few feet deeper and hang around their spawning tree with hopes of ambushing smaller prey. However, most crappies will move to weeded communities in about eight feet of water. But not just any weed will do. While a crappie will use any plant which offers protective cover when it is threatened, under normal circumstances it has a distinct preference for two members of the pondweed family: genus potamogeton. This family of marvelous plants has about the highest number of species of all submerged aquatic plants. And different species of the pondweed family are found in fresh, brackish, and salt waters and are distributed throughout most of the United States.

CLASPINGLEAF AND WHITESTEM PONDWEEDS

Within this family of plants is the group known to some anglers as "cabbage," "cabbage weeds," and "fish weeds." Depending on which angler you talk to, any of three or four different pondweeds might have these nicknames. Several species of fish are attracted to a number of the different pondweeds. Crappies, however are fairly selective in their choices of "cabbage."

A crappie's favorite choice of pondweed is the *Claspingleaf Pondweed* (P. Richardsonii), followed closely by the almost identical but deeper growing *Whitestem Pondweed* (P. Praelongus). Significantly, each of these pondweeds are usually found growing in firm and packed sandy bottoms, often the same type of bottom, although deeper, where bulrushes and other favored spawning areas are located. The convenient location of Claspingleaf and Whitestem pondweeds adjacent to solid bottomed areas makes them natural stopover spots for crappies en route to and from their spawning grounds.

*FOOTNOTE: The term "pondweed" refers to a specific genus of plants, not just any weed in the pond.

Pondweeds have not attained quite the growth at the onset of spawn that they will have by the time it's over. Therefore, pondweed is more likely to be used after the crappies have left their nests and are seeking a little deeper water. After spawning, crappies will hide in the shadows of these beautiful leafy plants, depending on water temperatures and the availability of prey, for about a two-week period.

Typically, pondweeds grow in communities. As few as two or three plants or as many as hundreds may be growing fairly close together. The most productive pondweeds to fish tend to be those growing fairly close together in clumps. Each of the clumps create a perfect low light ambush station and might hold several crappies. Crappies position themselves just a few feet below the tops of the plants sandwiched within the clumps and lie in wait for some unsuspecting prey (or your lure) to swim overhead.

Crappies are occasionally found in pondweed before and during spawning, especially in smaller wind-protected bays with access to deep water. The Whitestem pondweed (musky weed to some anglers) grows in water averaging 10 feet and deeper. Pre-spawn crappies prefer them over the Claspingleaf which usually grows in water of 8 feet deep or less. Heavy concentrations of Whitestem near spawning grounds can be loaded with large females. However, after spawning, crappies prefer Claspingleafs because crappies will remain relatively shallow (six to eight feet) until the more direct sun rays and temperatures of summer begin to drive them deeper.

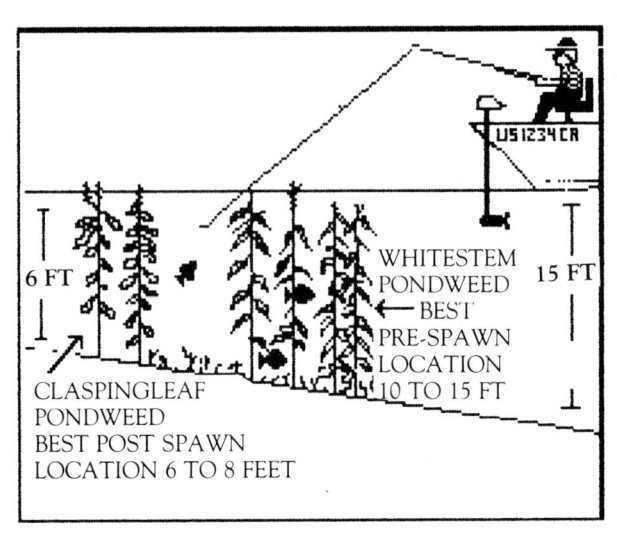

Find Whitestems or Claspingleafs in late spring or early summer and you're likely to find crappies. With little effort an angler can motor around a lake and soon learn if either of these plants are present. By wearing your polarized glasses you will be able to see the leafy stems and stalk-like spikes ("candles") just beneath the surface of the water. The candle tips of mature plants may barely stick through the water's surface, but the leaves are always below the water. The Claspingleaf leaves are usually shorter than 4 inches while those of the Whitestem may be over 4 inches. For angling purposes try not to be overly concerned about their taxonomic differences. Crappies aren't.

Claspingleaf and whitestem pondweeds are about the easiest of all crappie structures to fish. Your lure almost never hangs up and when it does it easily pulls free. You can wind drift over the pondweeds, trolling your lure through the tops, or cast and retrieve around each leafy clump from a distance. One post-spawn season day I caught (and released) so many crappies in the pondweed with the cast and retrieve method that I lost track of the number; I quit counting around 112 fish.

It's almost impossible to spook crappies when they're in pondweeds, so you can simply position your boat over the plants and jig your lure through the leaves. Usually, you can take fish from this structure throughout the day, but mornings and evenings are best.

To a lesser extent, crappies are also fond of Curled Pondweed (P. Crispus), a few of the Narrowleaf Pondweeds, Wild Celery, Chara, and a slimy little floating leaf plant called Water Shield. Even if you don't catch fish among them, they are lovely and interesting plants to study. One of the many joys of fishing is the satisfaction an angler

Post-spawn crappies taken from Claspingleaf Pondweed in six feet of water adjacent to bulrushes.

receives from the knowledge he gains about the mysterious aquatic world as he studies its plants to improve his angling skills. Just for the asking, most states' natural resource departments have publications on common aquatic vegetation which will assist the angler in identifying plants.

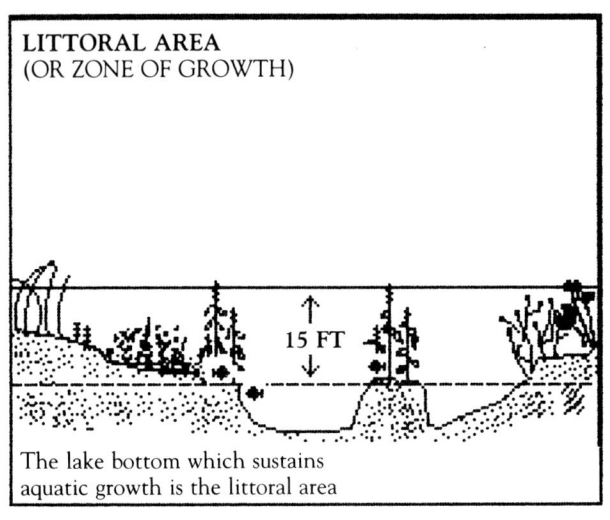

LITTORAL AREA
(OR ZONE OF GROWTH)

15 FT

The lake bottom which sustains aquatic growth is the littoral area

MIDDLE SUMMER AND FALL

For some anglers, summer is the worse time of the year to fish for crappies in lakes. They just aren't as easy to find because they seek deeper and cooler water. In very shallow lakes, this is an excellent time to concentrate your efforts alongside floating cattails, cypress tree roots, water hyacinths, or other shaded structures. Crappies must have shade since they cannot go deep to escape the sun. In deeper lakes, crappies will seek water averaging 14 to 17 feet down during midday and only move shallower as evening approaches. Why these depths? Mainly because the best combination of temperature comfort, light penetration (or lack of it), and pondweed cover is achieved. On the average, this is usually the depth where most vegetation will grow no deeper, depending on the clarity of the water.

Every lake has a portion of the water known as its Littoral Area or zone of growth. This is the title given to the area of a lake which basically contains all the rooted aquatic plants, fish foods, and generally, the fish themselves. With few exceptions, littoral areas with their rooted plants rarely exceed 17 feet deep in lakes with stable levels. For statistical purposes some states consider the littoral area of its waters to be everything shallower than 15 feet.

A littoral area can be 100% of some lakes if their entire bottoms are shallower than 15 feet. Included within a lakes littoral area are its shoreline shallows, the under, water portions of peninsulas (points), and those portions of sunken islands (humps) that are above the 15-

feet level. Of course many lakes will have some depths greater than 15 feet. The importance of all this lies in the fact that summer (and even early autumn) crappies will collect at the edge of littoral areas just at the depth where the rooted vegetation stops growing. This is usually 14 to 17 feet deep.

Not all edges of a lake's littoral area will attract crappies. Most notably, those which do have access to deeper water usually have pondweeds present and are physically shaped different from the surrounding area. For example, underwater points, humps, or breaks (sudden drop offs) near deeper water attracts crappies to their weed line's lower edges. With the aid of polarized sunglasses or an electronic depth finder, an angler can easily locate these edges.

USING A YARN MARKER

When fishing deep summer structure you should begin by tying a small piece of bright yarn on your line at approximately 15½ feet up from the end of your line where you have tied on a 1/32 ounce marabou jig. If you have a depth finder which gives you the exact depth at the edge of the weed line, then tie the yarn just at that measurement on your line. Trim the yarn so that it sticks out only about ⅛ of an inch on each side of the line. Make sure the yarn is tight enough around the line to prevent it from slipping up or down on its own.

The purpose of the yarn is to allow you to accurately and quickly strip line from your reel after each fish. This eliminates guesswork about whether or not you have let out the right amount of line to return to the depth where the fish are holding. Since crappies in deep summer water will be in water of 14 to 17 feet, you should set the marker somewhere in between (thus 15½ feet) until you know just exactly where to place the yarn. If you catch a fish before the yarn reaches the water, slide the colorful little marker down the line. If a crappie doesn't take the lure until the yarn disappears, raise the marker.

WEED LINES AND DROP OFFS

When fishing any deep water crappie structure an electric trolling motor is worth its weight in gold. With it, you will be able to slowly and precisely move along the edge of the weed line. It's especially crucial when the wind is blowing. The motor can keep you right on course or hold you in place if need be, without having to drop anchor.

To find the crappies, start out with your lure right on the bottom. Then simply move along the weed line as slowly as possible, raising the lure three to four feet up from the bottom and letting it fall back to the bottom again.

Important: As you lower the lure to the waiting fish, do it slowly so that no slack comes into the line.

If a large amount of slack (or a large bow) comes into your line as the lure descends, you will know that a fish has grabbed the bait. Set the hook immediately and take note of the location of your yarn marker. After you land your crappie you can adjust your yarn line marker as needed and drop the jig back into the water. As soon as you hook your first fish, drop a small marker buoy overboard. If you catch a few more next to the marker buoy, it might pay to drop anchor and fish the area thoroughly, even working the lure into the weed line a few feet.

TOPOGRAPHIC (CONTOUR) MAPS

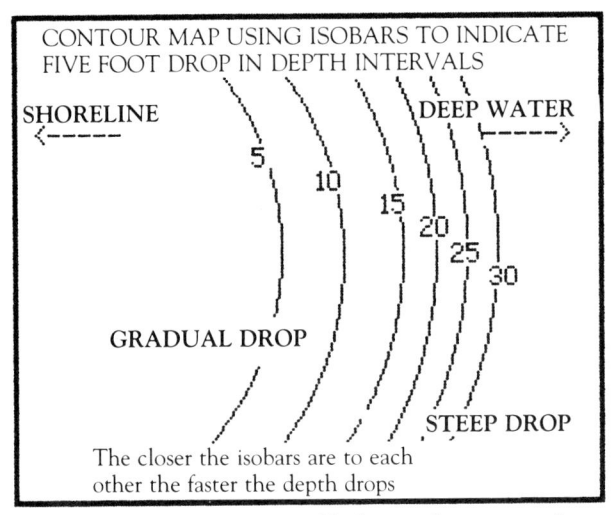

```
CONTOUR MAP USING ISOBARS TO INDICATE
FIVE FOOT DROP IN DEPTH INTERVALS
SHORELINE                    DEEP WATER
<-----                       |----->
          5
            10
              15
                20
                  25
                    30
     GRADUAL DROP

                        STEEP DROP
  The closer the isobars are to each
  other the faster the depth drops
```

Using contour maps an angler can quickly locate deep water drop offs, points, or underwater humps.

You will be able to save a lot of time looking for weed lines on drop offs with deep water nearby by consulting topographic (contour) maps. The changes in the contours of the earth beneath the water are indicated on these maps by lines known as isobars. When a map indicates isobars that are very close together this depicts an area of the lake where the depth of the water drops steeply. Isobars that are widely separated indicate gradual changes in depth.

UNDERWATER ISLANDS OR HUMPS

Contour maps are also useful for locating sunken islands (humps). Those underwater humps which have pondweeds growing on them will hold more crappies. But any hump near very deep water will draw fish. In most situations the most efficient way to fish them is to slowly wind drift over the area, trolling a jig directly beneath the boat until a crappie is caught. Drop a marker buoy overboard and continue to drift until you catch a second crappie. Then drop a second marker over at that location; fish thoroughly between the two markers and in the immediate area around them. If the hump is only 20 or 30 feet across, you can anchor down in the middle and work the entire area with the cast and retrieve approach.

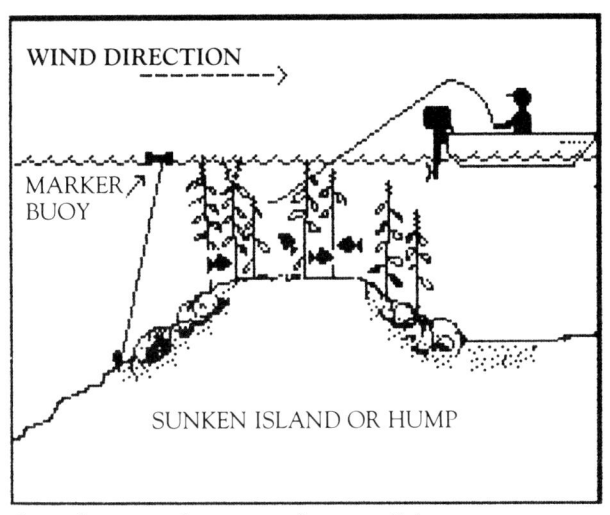

If you mark underwater humps with a small buoy, you can easily locate them again if the wind moves you away from the area.

POINTS OR UNDERWATER PENINSULAS

Few lakes have perfectly round shorelines. By contrast most have very irregular shores with the most striking irregularities being bays and peninsulas (points). Submerged points are especially productive areas for fishing. They extend the shallow littoral area into the lake and then taper off into deeper water. Sticking out into the water, they serve as a guide fence to shallow-water fish movement. Points become major travel routes for incoming crappies.

Because such submerged points are the first shallow water areas encountered by crappies during their twice daily low light movements from deep water to feed, fish are more likely to concentrate more thickly on them. Points are used as little rest stops as crappies ready themselves to spread out along the shallows in search of prey. Points are so productive that fisheries' managers usually place their sampling nets along such structures knowing that capturing fish on them is pretty much guaranteed.

Fishing points is just a matter of beginning on their shallow water end. Slowly jig your lure ever deeper with each gentle bounce down the tapering point until a concentration of crappies are found. During the summer and autumn this will be about 14 to 17 feet deep during the day but as shallow as three or four feet during low light conditions.

Remember to keep the slack out and watch for any unnatural line movement. When you do connect, set your line's yarn marker. Most of the fish on the entire point will be at the same depth. Points which contain pondweeds are the most productive.

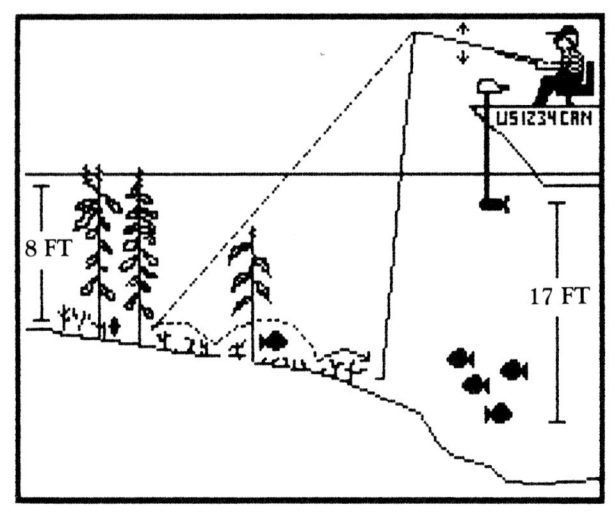

To fish points, slowly jig your lure down the slope until a concentration of crappies is found.

SUSPENDED FISH

During the hottest months of summer, crappies will sometimes concentrate in areas where there is absolutely no physical structure around to relate to other than each other. They will *suspend* at specific depths in the open water of larger lakes and reservoirs. In these suspended communities, there may be hundreds of crappies two or three feet deep holding in a tight formation sometimes covering an acre. Or there may be only 10 to 20 suspended crappies in such a formation.

Ideas among fishermen attempting to explain suspending behavior vary. The most likely possibility suggests that they are seeking a specific preferable temperature relative to the best low light condition available at the time. Crappies do like each other's company and seem drawn to each other. Once they've concentrated in large numbers they perhaps forget that they're unprotected in the open water. An illusion of protective cover is supplied by the presence of so many others as they virtually hide among themselves.

Suspended crappies can be found with electronic fish locators or by drifting your lure over deep water off points, weed lines, or humps. If you have located fish at a certain depth on one of the physical structures described above, chances are excellent that you will find suspended crappies at that same depth in open water. Again, your efforts should include searching in 14 to 17 feet of water.

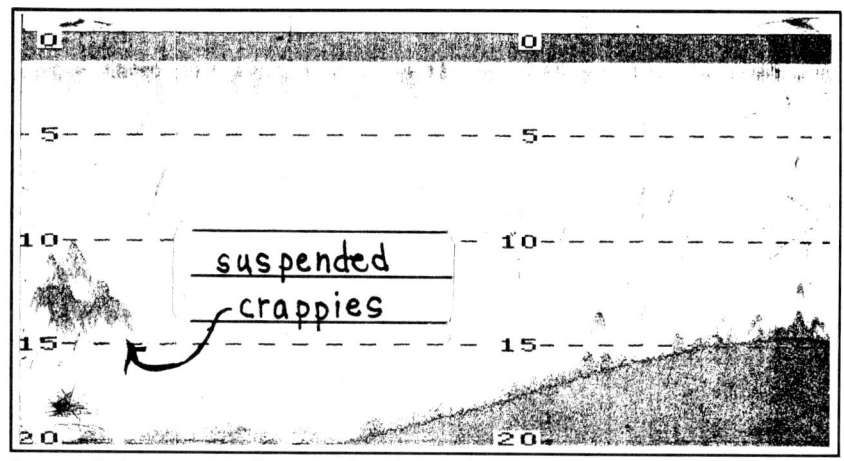

Suspended crappies will very often be at the same depth as their fellow crappies which are holding on a nearby structure. Note how the open-water suspended crappies on the left of this graph readout are about the same depth as those on the underwater hump shown on the right.

If your state fishing regulations allow it, your odds of locating suspended fish without the benefit of a fish locator will be increased by drift fishing a number of lures at different depths all at the same time. Whichever depth pays off first with more than one fish is the key depth for that area and type of structure.

Throughout this book I have emphasized the importance of moving extremely slowly. Sometimes the wind is so fierce that boat and line control is very difficult. The wind can drag you along too fast while you are trying to drift fish and will not allow your lightweight lure to sink to the desired depth. Even if you are anchored, your fishing line will catch the wind like a sail and keep your line bowed out with far too much slack in it. There really is only one way to overcome this: add extra weight.

If you must add extra weight at least do so by tying on another lure or two, spacing them at least 15 inches apart. If your state prohibits more than one hook or lure on a line, try fishing with a $\frac{1}{16}$th ounce jig. Although you will get less bites with the heavier lure, that's better than being defeated by the wind and not getting any fish at all. Some anglers will add a large sinker to their lines to reach their desired depth. If you happen to find a large school of very active fish, this method won't hurt too much, but if you are working only a few finicky crappies, the weight can distract them from the bait.

PORPOISING

Even if there is no such word as "porpoising," the connotation it suggests accurately describes a major pattern of crappie feeding behavior important to the angler. Most of the patterns above are primarily daytime crappie methods. But from late spring through early autumn, usually at sundown, the surface of a lake can all of a sudden seem to boil. Crappies can be seen bursting forth from the surface of the water by the hundreds. Occasionally some will come completely out of the water. Most crappies will come no farther out of the water than the tops of their backs and give the impression of imitating a porpoise.

When an angler witnesses this phenomenon he should move his boat as close as possible to the action and cast right into it. This behavior is caused by an insect hatch which is underway and the crappies are making the most of it. They follow the emerging insects right to the surface, sometimes coming partly out of the water in pursuit of their prey.

This feeding frenzy can last quite a while, moving about from place to place. An alert angler can follow the boils and really catch the fish. The best way to fish "porpoising" crappies is to swim your lure just beneath the surface. An angler with a fly rod and marabou streamers will catch more fish.

Summer and even autumn crappie fishing is most difficult to master because the angler doesn't have the same visual cues he has during the spring when he knows that most timber, reeds, and shade structure will hold crappies. In very shallow lakes the spring patterns can produce fish all year long. In deep lakes, however, you have to change your approach. Set you mind on fishing all the points, humps, and drop offs. Then it's just a matter of commitment to sticking to your plan of attack. If you concentrate your efforts on the weed lines in 14 to 17 feet of water you will catch fish.

River Crappies
"Beside Still Waters"

...BESIDES STILL WATERS;
HE RESTORES MY SOUL

RIVERS

Of all the varieties of crappie structure to fish, rivers are my first love. One of the appealing things about rivers is that they can be fished almost as successfully from shore as from a boat. I've spent many joyous hours fishing from the banks of the beautiful St. Croix River which forms much of the Minnesota-Wisconsin boundary. On lake shore, anglers are pretty much limited to spring fishing with a few exceptions. However, river fishermen can usually find shore fishing productive spring, summer, and early fall in northern states and throughout the year in the south.

River fishing can be most challenging, because very little of the water in a river holds fish. This chapter will help the angler to predict fairly well where to locate river crappies. As we discuss river fishing, please note that the same types of conditions which apply to rivers will apply to larger creeks and streams. In fact, occasionally, many smaller streams, perhaps no more than two or three feet across and a foot or so deep, will contain transient (traveling) crappies in the spring. The pattern for locating them will also be the same as for a river.

STILL WATERS - OR EDDIES

If a river or stream has crappies, three main elements must be present to some degree for a location to be an outstanding crappie hot spot: still water next to fast water near deep water. The natural flow of the river will in most cases provide the necessary fast water. This element is the least one to worry about; it's almost always present. Deep water can usually be discovered fairly easily also. The river crappie angler must concentrate his efforts then on locating quiet or nearly still water next to the faster water which results from an interruption of the river's flowage. This type of still water is known as an "eddy."

The best river crappie locations will be in very still water next to faster moving and deeper water.

An eddy is a current of water which moves contrary to the direction of the main current, usually in a circular motion. Eddies which create powerful whirlpools hold little value to crappie fishermen. The best ones are those larger slow moving pools where crappies can escape the tiring rush and roar of the main current. In fact, most river fish including minnows use eddies as rest stops. Of course, nothing could make a crappie happier. He can rest and eat at the same time. The bigger the contrast between the fast water and the still water the better.

Even though rivers may be wide, deep, and long, very little of that water is actually used by crappies except as a travel route to get from one eddy to another. Fast water becomes a difficult barrier which crappies prefer to avoid. Instead, they congregate in still water areas. Crappies are naturally stimulated by flowing water. They instinctively know that food is plentiful in the pools which form within and alongside the main flow of a river or stream. They swim along the paths of least resistance until they locate the quiet areas. There they rest and wait for careless minnows to move through or perhaps insect larvae to be swept into the pool.

Try to think of a river as a great, long, food conveyer belt which travels past hundreds of resting and dining spots for hungry crappies. In lakes, as we have seen, the best time of day to fish is during low light hours. To a great extent it's the same for rivers. However, lake fish are more spread out and have more choices of structures to use.

River crappies have one basic structure: still water. And because there are likely to be some crappies at this structure 24 hours a day, the odds of catching them during midday hours are also excellent. Walleyes, white bass, and small mouths also rely on eddies for resting and feeding stations.

The demand and competition for good eddies can be intense in rivers with large populations of crappies. In such rivers, fish can be caught all day long from many eddies, especially in the spring. Should you find an eddy with only a few crappies, move on to another for awhile. Return later and try again. Chances are pretty good that more crappies will have moved in to replace those you have already taken.

How are eddies formed? How do you know where to look for them? Really, almost any object placed in the direct route of the main flow of water will create an eddy. Wing dams, sandbars, boulders, fallen timber, bridge piles, islands, and even the flowing water colliding with itself will create quiet spots of still water.

IRREGULAR SHORELINE PROTRUSIONS

It was in just such a pool that I caught (and released) 150 crappies in an hour while refining the 1½ inch length to the marabou jig. This type of eddy can be created by sand bars that stick out from shore, huge boulders lying along the shore, peninsulas, and wing dams. These barriers force flowing water around them on one side, creating water pools with little or no movement immediately behind them.

The most productive way to fish these pools is to cast and retrieve across them at as many angles as possible. By holding your rod tip up and retrieving slowly, the lure will swim just beneath the surface helping to avoid snags. If that does not pay off, try retrieving a little slower with each cast allowing the lure to sink a little deeper. If you start losing too many lures on the bottom you can add a bobber. Fly rods are devastatingly effective here as the light marabou flies almost never snag.

SHORELINE TIMBER

Shoreline timber eddies are formed by fallen trees and the massive root systems of living trees like those of the cypress. This structure is fantastic in rivers or creeks with moderate to slow moving water not only because of the still water which develops behind them, but also because of the shade or low light condition they produce.

This pattern is fished pretty much the same as on lakes. If fishing from a boat, approach downed timber from the up river side. Allow your boat to drift against the timber, thus preventing the flow of the river from taking you downstream. If you are fishing in states with poisonous snakes, you will certainly want to look over the tree carefully before you bump into it.

RIVER CRAPPIES
"BESIDE STILL WATERS"

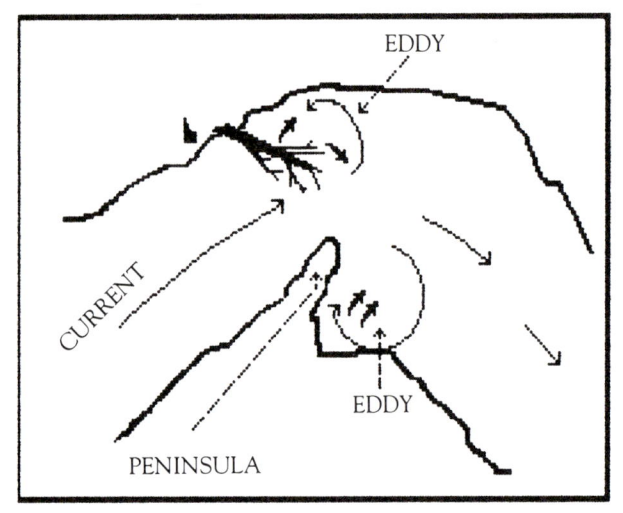

Eddies are found on the down river side of objects which stick out from shore including sand bars, peninsulas, and fallen trees. Crappies collect in these calm water areas.

The eddies created by fallen shoreline timber are outstanding places to fish river crappies.

It's a good idea to have both a very short and extremely long pole rigged up with a jig. The short one allows you to yo-yo the lure right alongside the boat into the timber; the longer pole allows you to reach or poke your lure through the limbs so you can lower it into places where casting is impossible. Shore anglers can be very effective reaching downed timber with very long jigger poles. These poles are especially effective tools in and around cypress trees.

ISLANDS AND VERY LARGE BOULDERS

Eddies always occur on the down river end of each side of islands and huge boulders as the water rushes around the edges. This pattern is fished by casting on the up river side of the structure and allowing the current to wash the lure into the eddy. Waiting crappies will do the rest. Underwater boulders will even form bottom eddies.

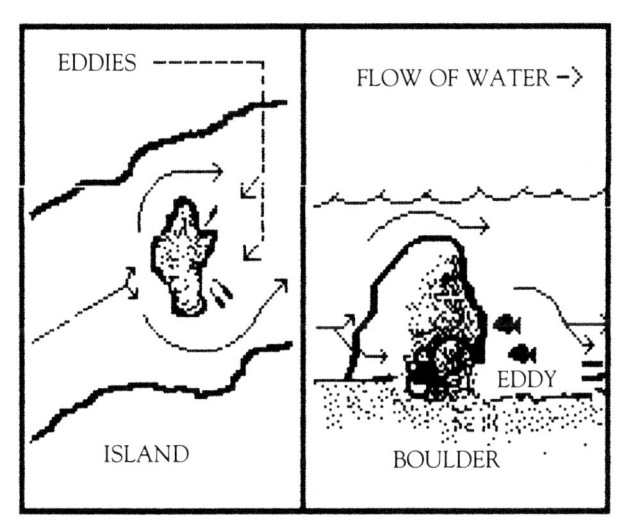

When fishing boulders or islands, cast into the fast-flowing water and allow the lure to be swept into the eddy.

BRIDGE PILES OR SUPPORTS

On the down river side of these structures, still water results from the bridge support interfering with the main flow of water. Those supports which are elliptical and are set at an angle to the flow of water will hold more fish than perfectly round pilings. Bridge pilings usually have a secondary tier of larger unseen foundations which will hold fish. Bridges also provide shade.

RIVER CRAPPIES
"BESIDE STILL WATERS"

Fishing friend and fellow conservation officer Kermit Piper displays a nice catch of crappies taken in the eddies of bridge pilings.

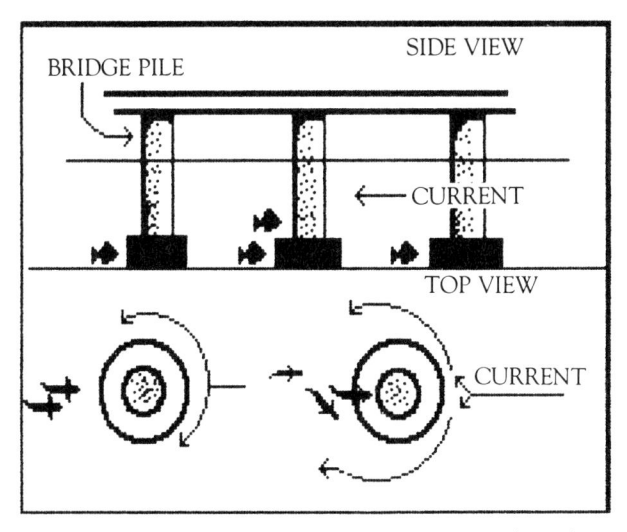

Bridge pilings are especially attractive to crappies, providing them with calm and shaded water.

Bridge supports are best fished by allowing the lure to wash into the eddy or by moving your boat into the eddy and jigging directly into the still water. In the spring and again in the fall these structure become heat collectors. Crappies and white bass will snuggle up to them for warmth, so you should place your lure (or bait) as close to the supports as possible. To take walleyes behind pilings, allow the jig to sink right to the bottom and yo-yo it up and down a few times.

SHARP S-CURVES ON DEEP RIVER BENDS

As rivers turn sharp corners they can create two types of eddies: an inside curve eddy and an outside bend eddy. The inside curve works on the same principle as any water-obstacle eddy. As the water rushes around the inside curve or point, there is an area immediately behind the point of still water. This can often be an excellent area for fish. However, I've found that the outside turn of sharp bends will hold more crappies, providing that the bend has very deep water adjacent to it.

An unusual phenomenon occurs as a river rushes against an outside bank before it makes its turn. As it attempts to turn the corner, back pressure is generated by trapped water piling upon itself. It careens to one side, and that motion of the water turns into a barrier. A buffer zone of pressed upon water develops between the main flow of the river and the water just along the shore. The trapped water next to shore behind the buffer often holds crappies. These areas may be only a few square yards or they might cover an acre of water.

RIVER CRAPPIES
"BESIDE STILL WATERS"

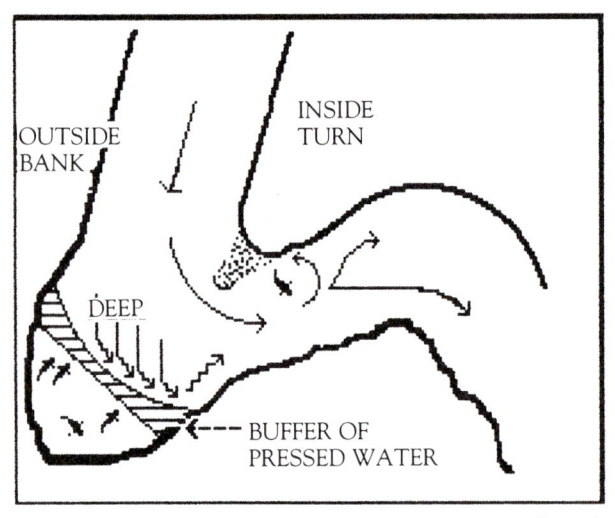

The outside turns of sharp river bends can create unusual pockets of calm water which crappies seek.

This river crappie greedily struck both jigs which were fished in tandem in an outside, deep water, s-curve bend.

Deep river bend crappies are found by slowly trolling tandem jigs through the deeper parts of the river bend eddy or by casting and retrieving along the shore in the shallows. If the s-curve pocket is quite large, you should mark the location of your first fish with a marker buoy. Then concentrate your efforts in that area.

TAILWATERS

These are the waters found at the end and on the sides of the very fast-moving water from dams, waterfalls, power plant outlets, white water, and feeder creeks and streams. Crappies can sense those areas where a body of water receives an inrush of faster water. In those spots where the very force of the water and sometimes the height of the structure prevents movement up river, injured baitfish and other creatures accumulate and create feeding opportunities for the merciless crappies and other game fish. Crappies will hold in the calmest sections of tail waters, while the other game fish are more likely to be somewhat closer to the fast water.

In the heat of summer, crappies will seek the eddies of frothy white water because of the comfort of cooler temperatures and the excellent concentration of oxygen generated by the movement of water cascading over rocks and through narrows. The base of waterfalls will hold crappies for the same reasons. Extreme caution should be exercised when fishing near dams, especially low head dams which have taken many lives. When fishing these areas, please observe all the posted safety rules. Extra care should always be taken when angling anywhere in rivers.

Extreme caution should be exercised when fishing near dams, especially low head dams which have taken many lives.

All of the illustrated eddy patterns will be more productive areas to fish if there happens to be a combination of two or more of them in the same location. For example, an ideal spot would be a fallen tree laying in an eddy just behind another structure sticking out from shore near very deep water. Add shade from a moored boat, dock, log jam, or floating vegetation and you will find the spot even more productive.

During spring, summer, and fall, rainstorms more than any other factor will affect the quality of river crappie fishing. Heavy rainfall causes two major problems for the angler. First, heavy rains cause silting in the river. As the river clouds up from silt, sight feeding fish simply can't see your bait or lure. Second, the changes in river levels after a rainstorm will change the complex network of familiar shoreline eddies, causing many of those spots so productive the day before to disappear.

Among the instincts gifted to a crappie by its Creator surely must be the good sense to lie low during increasing violent water speeds and rising river levels during and after storms. After all, crappies are not streamlined or powerful like a trout or a smallmouth bass. They must stick even tighter to their protective, less turbulent, bottom eddies during torrential water movements or be dashed against rocks or timber. They will avoid the rapidly changing, treacherous shorelines at such times. When the river returns to normal, excellent crappie fishing will resume.

Storms aren't the only reasons for rapid river level changes. River levels are also affected by the release of water from reservoir dams. Existing eddies will disappear within minutes and new ones will be created as levels change. The release of reservoir water rarely creates a silting problem like rainstorms and almost never increases water speed down river for very far. It does add a challenge to the river angler who might be fishing below such structures. Not only will he have to be flexible enough to locate a new eddy as the water rises, he will most assuredly seek higher ground with the good sense his Creator gave him.

Fancy lure action is not necessary when fishing rivers. In fact it might hurt your chances. Most rivers have enough water coloration to make fishing for sight feeders a deliberately slow art. Jerking or jigging your lure too vigorously will not give crappies the time to see and take the offering. Allow the rivers current to give the marabou its lifelike strike-enticing action. When fishing rivers you should take along several lures. Not only will the fickle waters sweep your lures onto snags, but occasionally other species of huge fish will grab your lures and simply keep going.

There are three main ideas to keep in mind when fishing rivers. First, fish eddies, those slow moving pools located next to deep and fast water. Second, keep changing locations whenever the fish stop hitting. Experiment by moving up and down the river, locating as many eddy situations as possible to find more crappies. Then try the same ones again after awhile. And finally, cover every square inch of an eddy with your lure. Often there are unseen boulders, trees, or other secondary structures beneath the surface of the water within the eddy which will create low light situations causing the fish to concentrate in a specific spot. Good luck!

Crappies Through the Ice

WINTER ICE FISHING

For the most part, winter ice fishing has little in common with open-water angling. First, the equipment is quite different. Fish houses, snowmobiles, and four-wheel drive trucks replace boats. Fish sticks replace rods and reels, and live bait now becomes very important.

Second, mobility is very restricted, depending on the snow cover and ice conditions. The freedom of movement enjoyed with a boat is gone. Despite that, being willing to move about during the winter is just as important as it is for open-water angling. But drilling fishing holes in the ice isn't exactly a labor of love. If an angler doesn't find fish after the first few holes, he soon gets fed up with drilling. He stays put catching little or no fish and finally gives up altogether and goes home.

Finally, the time of day one fishes for crappies in the winter becomes critically important. Knowing where to drill your first holes is not as important as knowing when to fish and how deep to set your bait.

TIME OF DAY AND DEPTH

There is absolutely no doubt that the best time of day for winter ice fishing for crappies is during low light or even dark hours. About an hour before sunset crappies really go on the prowl as they move from their deep water winter sanctuaries and head for the shallows in search of minnows or other organisms.

Once you've selected an area to start angling you should be able to locate the exact depth of the fish with an electronic fish finder. If you don't have a fish finder, take your thermos, walk over to the nearest frost-covered fishermen that is catching fish, and coax the depth information from with a cup of hot chocolate. Try to determine the exact depth within inches that the crappies are being caught. If your new frozen friend is willing, ask him to pull up one of his lines and measure it from hook to bobber. Well-meaning anglers might just give you an estimate, not realizing the importance of being very specific.

A handy way to measure the depth at which one is fishing is to stretch sections of fishing line out between your nose and the tips of your fingers. If you do this off to your side, each section of line will equal almost exactly half your height. A person who is six feet tall should have a side reach of three feet. If he pulls up five arm sections of line from his bobber to his hook then he is fishing 15 feet deep.

As soon as you catch your first fish, note the exact depth and adjust your bait to that level. This is notably different from warmer water periods when you must place your lure or bait just in front and slightly above the crappie; during the winter try to place it exactly at the same level. Most winter crappies simply do not wish to come up more than a few inches for bait. In fact, winter crappies can be slow to hit even when your bait is placed right in front of them.

I've spent countless hours studying crappies through the holes of my darkened fish house floor. Sometimes they will take the bait immediately and at other times they will ease up to it, stare at it endlessly, and then swim on. I've found that I can increase the number of bites by frequently, but slowly, raising the bait and letting it fall slowly back. This will often provoke an immediate attack by the crappie.

About two to three hours after sunset, some of the crappies which moved through earlier will come through again returning to their sanctuary. They won't necessarily be swimming at the same depth as earlier; they'll probably be shallower. Here again an electronic fish locator is a valuable tool in this situation. However, without one an angler should be constantly testing various depths by raising and lowering the bait in the hole until fish are again being caught. Once again adjust your bobber to that level. About an hour each side of sunrise and to some degree throughout the night, crappies will make additional shallow water movements and can readily be caught at this new level.

LOCATING CRAPPIES THROUGH THE ICE

As strange as it might seem, you will find winter crappies in about the same locations as during the mid-summer, only a little deeper. And, too, over the decades enough anglers have discovered excellent winter crappies spots that there will almost always be numerous fish houses located over these areas. This is just the opposite from open water angling where one should never follow the crowd.

If there is one winter location likely to be more productive than others, it would be the large underwater points (peninsulas) which taper off into very deep water. These can be readily located with the contour maps discussed earlier. And in the absence of other anglers or without the benefits of contour maps, you can still find these points. I always go to the largest peninsulas evident on the shoreline. I then walk out on the ice several yards until I think I have reached a depth of 17 to 20 feet. Sometimes this can be fairly accurately estimated by looking at the slope of the peninsula before it enters the water.

If the slope of the peninsula is steep above the waterline, it most likely will drop off rapidly into deeper water fairly close to shore. If it tapers gradually before it enters the water, it will probably taper at the same angle beneath the waterline. You will have to walk out farther from shore to reach deep water.

When you have located bottom depths of 17 to 20 feet, begin by fishing six inches from the bottom. Move your bait up six inches at a time until you find the exact depth the crappies are holding. If you do not locate fish over these depths, move to even deeper water and try the same procedure again. During midwinter, crappies have been caught over 40 feet deep. If fishing over deeper bottoms does not pay off, try moving up the underwater point over a shallower bottom.

These points obstruct the migration routes of minnows and other swimming food sources, causing them to bunch up around these natural barriers. That attracts crappies. As stated earlier, because these barriers reach out into the deep water they are usually the first areas crappies encounter during their feeding runs. As they move from deep water to feed they will travel along the points looking for prey. And they will almost always use the same routes.

Depending on how near you have positioned yourself to one of their travel routes, you might have only five or six fish move under your holes or you could have fifty or sixty. Whatever the number, they won't be there long.

As crappies begin to move through the area, it's extremely important to keep fishing. Resist all temptation to waste time. Immediately drop a freshly baited hook back through the ice after each fish while the crappies are still there.

If you happen to have several pre-drilled holes you will be able to catch a few more fish by following them. You can determine the direction they are going by the direction your bobber travels as it is pulled through the hole. If the bobber is pulled to the north, the fish are moving to the north, and so on. Using this technique, it's possible to discover a great treasure of crappies which will allow you access to excellent fishing opportunities at any hour of the day.

WINTER SANCTUARIES

Crappies have a tendency to "bunch up" or suspend in tight groups during the winter. For some unexplained reason, winter concentrations of crappies will select a certain area of a given lake and seem to use that area as a home base, leaving it only to go on feeding sprees. Some anglers refer to such a location of fish as a *sanctuary*. Larger lakes will have several such sanctuaries.

How do you locate a sanctuary? It's really quite simple. While fishing midmorning hours you will more than likely be catching crappies that are returning to their sanctuary. Note the direction your bobber travels as you hook your first two or three crappies. Drill a hole a few feet in that direction. If the fish continue to move off in that direction follow them.

When you have arrived at a place where the bobber goes straight down into the hole or barely goes any where, you are above the sanctuary. This spot may be no larger than the size of a car, but it can hold hundreds of fish. And at any time of the day or night there will be hungry fish at that location. Locating sanctuaries takes time and hard work, but once found will yield abundantly all winter.

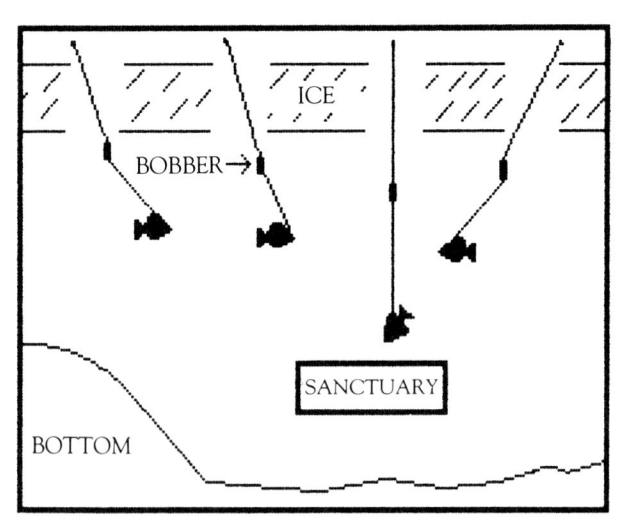

Drill new holes in the direction of the bobber movement until you've found a hole where the bobber goes straight down. At this point you will find a deep water crappie sanctuary.

Should you find fish in shallow water it's critical to move about on the ice as little as possible or you might scare them away. Commercial ice fishermen actually herd frightened fish into waiting nets they have placed under the ice by pounding on the ice with objects as they walk abreast toward the nets or by driving mufflerless snowmobiles to and fro, frightening the fish ever closer to the nets with each lap. It's actually the movement on the ice and not so much the noise which frightens the fish.

Winter fishing presents quite a challenge. Yet successful ice fishing for crappies can be easily accomplished by following a few simple rules. First, fish morning and evening around sunrise and sunset and an hour each side of these events. During the winter this is more critical than at any other time of the year. Next, try to establish from others or with an electronic fish finder the exact depth where crappies are holding. Then locate points near deep water or sharp drop-offs. Crappies should be nearby. Finally, use live minnows or wax worms for bait; the smaller the minnow the better.

ICE FISHING EQUIPMENT

One of the appealing things about ice fishing equipment is its simplicity and low cost. Most ice fishermen use small wooden handled fiberglass fishing rods about two feet long with about 50 or 60 feet of line wound around pegs on the handle of the rods. They usually have a large pail to carry their fish and equipment and to sit on once their holes are drilled. They'll have a few # 6 hooks, some BB sized split shot (lead weights), bobbers, and bait. And of course they will have something to make a hole in the ice.

The following is a checklist of ice fishing equipment for catching crappies. Occasionally, you will hook other species just as you will during open water fishing. And indeed most of these items would be needed no matter what you might be after. But the following recommendations are for crappies.

ICE AUGERS

To make holes in the ice, the winter fishermen can choose between four basic styles of hole makers. The more hardy souls still use ice chisels. And a few still use the old spoon-shaped ice bore. Most anglers are now using the screw-shaped ice augers. These newer style augers have rapidly grown in popularity because of the ease with which they drill holes. Still with very thick ice and after drilling several holes looking for fish, even these revolutionary tools can wear you down. The most advance type of drills are the gas or electric powered augers.

One winter, I was complaining to a fishing friend about how tiring and time wasting it can be to drill holes. "Why don't you buy a gas powered auger?" He asked. "After all, as often as you ice fish you'll probably use it as much as you do your fishing boat in the summer. And the auger will sure cost much less than your boat did."

He was right, of course. I began to think of all the time I could save with a power auger and the increased ability to move about looking for better spots; so I priced one. I discovered that it was indeed relatively inexpensive when compared to the money I had poured into my fishing boat and all its extra doodads and frills that I'd talked myself into believing I needed. I decided to get one, and it has added many extra hours of fun to my winter fishing.

ICE SKIMMER

Once you've drilled your hole in the ice you are going to need to clean all the crushed ice shavings from the hole. Also, on days where the temperatures are below freezing the surface of the water in your hole will keep freezing over. The thin film of ice which forms in the hole will freeze your bobber into place, preventing it from signaling the faint bite of a crappie. You must constantly skim the forming ice from the hole. Failure to do this is the most common mistake made by winter panfishermen. Your ice skimmer can also serve as a minnow dipper.

ICE FISHING RODS

Most ice crappie fishermen use the tiny ice fishing rods (jig sticks). These rods are not equipped with reels because there would be no way to reel in the line beyond the bobber which is often 17 feet or more above the hook. You'd never get the hook in. The bobber is obviously too large to fit through the rod ferrules or the reel's mechanism. Yet, ice fishing for crappies is usually best accomplished with the use of bobbers. Winter crappies bite so softly that a bobber might be the only way to detect the presence of a fish. These practical inexpensive reel-less ice fishing rods store the excess line and the much needed bobber on pegs which stick out of the handles.

It's interesting that winter fishermen even use rods at all because they almost always fish by hand lining. Once a fish is hooked the angler hauls up the catch by pulling the line up hand over hand. That's no big deal when you're fishing shallow. But when the crappies are really deep and you've pulled 20 or 30 feet of line up onto the ice (remember, there's no reel to hold the extra line) the freezing temperatures makes the wet overlapping line stick to itself and everything else it touches, giving new meaning to the phrase "tangled mess." Actually, the wimpy little flexible ice fishing poles should be used because their slender tips will yield more when fighting fish. Their flexibility will prevent the crappie angler from losing fish.

An ideal arrangement would be to attach a reel which has an adjustable drag to one of the little rods. That can be accomplished easily enough, but you still need to add a bobber. But how do you combine the rod, reel, and bobber so that you can fish deep water? The solution to this problem must allow the bobber to easily slide down the line as you reel in your fish, but must then conveniently return to the exact depth setting you were using when you hooked the fish. With such a sliding bobber rig, you can add a reel to your ice rod and avoid the aggravating hassle of your line lying all over the ice. Various tackle manufacturers have developed sliding *slip bobber* rigs. One style clearly stands out as being superior.

This type of adjustable depth slip bobber rig consists of a small bead and a oversized knot of heavy string wound around a short piece of tubing. This rig can be purchased at most bait shops. The instructions for using them are usually on the packaging, but I've included them here to give you an idea of what to expect.

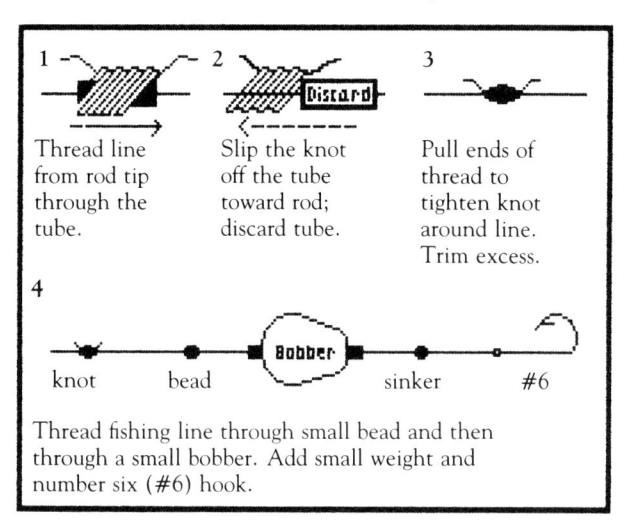

```
1                    2                    3
Thread line          Slip the knot        Pull ends of
from rod tip         off the tube         thread to
through the          toward rod;          tighten knot
tube.                discard tube.        around line.
                                          Trim excess.

4
knot      bead         Bobber       sinker        #6

Thread fishing line through small bead and then
through a small bobber. Add small weight and
number six (#6) hook.
```

Adjust the knot to whatever depth you decide to fish. On catching a fish simply reel up the fish. The bobber will slide down along the line instead up jamming up against the rod tip. Bait your hook again and drop it back into the hole. The weight of the baited hook and split shot will pull the sinking line back down sliding through the buoyant bobber. The line will slip through the bobber and bead until they come to rest against the knot tied around the line. You will then be fishing again at the same depth. To change depths, just move the knot in either direction to the desired depth.

LINE, BOBBERS, HOOKS, AND BAIT

The best recommended fishing line for winter crappies is still four pound test line. You will have to be extra cautious with your line on the ice. Sharp edges on some of the scooped out ice around fishing holes can cut your line. As you skim the reforming ice from the water's surface, try to scoop a little water with it and allow this to drip on the edges of your fishing hole. The water will melt down the sharper edges.

When selecting ice bobbers you will find that the blaze orange or bright yellow ones are easier to see contrasted against the white sides or the hole. I prefer the styrofoam type because they are unbreakable.

There are two effective types of hooks for ice crappies. Plain number six hooks or teardrops of sizes #6 through #10. Teardrops are small, colorful, weighted hooks which can be fished with minnows or wax worms and are available at bait shops. They need no other weight to take the bait down. Should you decide to use minnows, it's best to hook them in the manner demonstrated earlier. Always remember to use the smallest minnows possible. Wax worms are simply thread onto the hook from end to end.

Minnows will provide their own crappie-attractive action. But teardrops with "waxies" will have to be frequently danced up and down to attract attention. On some days, crappies will prefer one of these baits over the other. If you live in a state that allows the use of two lines in the winter, you can bait up one of each until you discover which they like best.

If you have determined that you are fishing the right depth but aren't getting bites, lift the bait several inches above the fish and very slowly allow it to sink back. If your line goes limp in the hole then one of the fish has risen to meet the bait and has it. Set the hook! Try to estimate the distance the fish rose for the bait and temporarily adjust your bobber to that depth. It might work again.

FISH HOUSES: PROTECTION FROM THE ELEMENTS

The fish house is probably the most expensive equipment the ice angler will invest in. While some are cheaply constructed, many of them cost hundreds of dollars to build. Some have all the comforts of home, including bunk beds, stoves for cooking and heat, television, and wall-to-wall carpeting. The angler can fish in total comfort. Mobility and maintenance are, of course, problems for the larger structures and this has given rise to the popularity of portable fish-houses.

Almost every kid has made a little club house or tree house to retreat into a world of make believe and fantasy, a private place to day dream, to think, and to hope. I believe that the thousands of fish houses that spring up on the winter ice of northern lakes may be, in a sense, little tree houses on the ice. If this theory is true, this then is an amazing phenomenon when you consider that the state of Minnesota alone registers nearly one hundred thousand fish houses annually.

Of all the various personalities of anglers that I've met, it seems that ice fishermen in fishhouses are less likely to grumble when the fishing is less than desirable. Perhaps the reason lies in the fact that fishing is not their only reason for being there. Many of the houses placed on the ice become little homes away from home; some are places to entertain friends or a spot to relax and escape from the worries of the world. Fish house ice fishing is excellent therapy. And when fish are caught, that's even better.

ICE SAFETY

Every year victims are lost through thin ice. It is especially heartbreaking when an innocent child is involved. However anxious you might be to begin your ice fishing season, please heed the warnings of local authorities about thin ice.

Most states provide excellent reading materials which deal with ice safety. Ice fishermen should study these carefully. First ice and late season ice are probably the most dangerous. When you begin to hear the late winter/early spring ice warnings, this is an excellent time to start tying up a good supply of $\frac{1}{32}$ ounce jigs and daydreaming about open water.

CONSERVATION: A CALL TO STEWARDSHIP

FRAGILE:HANDLE WITH CARE

The Creator has lovingly turned over his most glorious handiwork to our care and use. Surely, any work of art reflects the personality of its maker and keeps all who would gaze upon it mindful of the artist. That our natural resources are beautiful and abundantly given, then, should come as no surprise. Waste, disrespect, and abuse are actions that can forfeit that trust so freely given to us because they distort the beauty and purpose of the gift. Our duties to wisely care for nature must not be forsaken, for not only could we lose forever the gift, but also a chance to know the grace of the Giver.

A Conservation Officer waits in the dark. He lies hidden in the newly budded bushes near a lake which has been set aside as a state fish refuge. The fish from this lake are netted out by officials and used as brood stock to replenish hundreds of other lakes for the benefit of many sportsmen. Recently, someone with little regard for conservation efforts has selfishly molested the fisheries nets on several occasions. Hundreds of valuable egg ripe fish have been stolen.

The spring night is cold, damp, and lonely. Will the fish thieves come? The officer has been vigilantly waiting night after night, dividing the hours between two separate trouble spots. On this night, he is working alone. The only sounds he hears are the relentless chorus of frogs in a nearby marsh and an occasional crinkle of the cellophane wrapping on the flattened sandwich stuffed in his coat pocket. His thoughts frequently turn to his sleeping family who sees very little of him this time of the year.

He's alone because his neighboring wardens are having similar problems. Violators are night-spearing vulnerable fish on their spawning runs in creeks and streams around the state. There is no one to spare on this night to help out. If the violators come, will there be problems? He has already double checked his self-defense equipment to reassure himself. He checks it again. He knows there are real dangers to an officer in this situation. It has happened before. Two game wardens from his state were shot to death over fish (bullheads). Other wardens have been speared, clubbed, run over, and even mutilated.

Occasionally, an officer is overly cautious. But he knows the public will be tolerant of this. I shall never forget the extraordinary meeting I had with a certain gentleman about 2 am one misty night. I had received a complaint that he was fishing way into the night and taking over his limit. On finding his vehicle parked near the lake, I staked it out.

Within half of an hour he returned, placed something in the trunk, and started his motor. I approached his vehicle with my flashlight pointing into his car not knowing what to expect; I identified myself and asked him to step from his car. Would he have too many fish? What kind of a person was he? Was there someone else with him that I hadn't seen? If he was a violator, would he overreact to being checked? An officer is trained to consider these questions when approaching a possible violator at night.

The very moment I placed my light on him his right hand quickly moved from his steering wheel to some object lying on the front seat. "Take your light off me," he said in a rather stressful voice. What was he reaching for? Why did he want me to take my light away? I stepped back. Again he insisted that I take my light away but this time with more gruffness in his voice. Was this the moment that every officer dreads?

I very firmly demanded that he place both of his hands back on the steering wheel and made it clear that in no way was I going to turn my flashlight away. "Please officer," he pleaded. "I've got a glass eye and I would like the dignity of putting it in before I step out to talk to you." Try if you will to put yourself in my position at that moment. As it turned out, his request had been sincere. Furthermore, he was not in violation of any fishing regulation and he graciously accepted my explanation for my being very cautious.

Now, back to the young officer guarding the fish refuge. He decided to change locations after an hour or so wait. Silently, he slipped through the darkness to his alternate problem area. As he listened for sounds and searched with his night vision scope, he discovered two poachers illegally taking fish. His vigilance and courage were rewarded. And, thankfully, he was able to apprehend and bring them to justice without any problems. This time!

This is one of thousands of cases successfully handled each year by fish and game enforcement officers across the nation trying to conserve the natural resources for all to enjoy. On this particular night the officer was fortunate to stop the poaching before too many fish had been killed. Only six brooder walleyes and about two dozen brooder crappies, some of which approached two pounds, had been unlawfully taken. Yet, with the pre-spawn death of those walleyes, close to 400,000 eggs were lost forever. The roe from the crappies would have produced over 1,000,000 eggs.

Managing the natural resources properly is a complex affair involving a variety of agencies each with their respective specialty. The conservation enforcement officer mentioned above was by no means the only resource specialist involved directly with those fish. Dedicated fisheries specialists and biologists plan and carry out intense measures to insure quality fishing experiences for sportsmen. And certainly there are other agencies too numerous to list that contribute to fisheries' management.

Sportsmen must certainly be applauded for it is their tax money and license purchases that makes resource management possible. Therefore, it is the sportsmen that are being robbed when poachers arrogantly pillage and waste the harvest of pond and field, leaving an ungrateful bloody trail of fur, feathers, and fins.

They appreciate that the wild beast and fish were meant not only to nourish the body but the spirit as well. If this were not so, how would one explain the pervasive numbers of wildlife, fishing, and conservation organizations that exist? Most of the groups are made up exclusively of sportsmen who work together in a spirit of stewardship solely for the purpose of protecting the interest of fish and wildlife.

Individuals often display this same spirit. I am reminded of a hunter who passed up an easy shot at a lame deer and placed his own coat over it during a violent thunderstorm while he sent his hunting partner to find the warden so it could be taken into care, or a fisherman I once met who releases each of his large fish with a prayer that a small child might catch it next.

Those who hunt and fish with reverence and dignity and dedicate themselves to conservation principles have answered a call to stewardship. But unfortunately, their efforts are mocked by poachers who have no regard for the work of the steward, the purpose of the creature, or the generosity of the *Giver.*

Make no mistake about it. There is a battle underway. The underhanded approach of the poacher does not bring with it high visibility. But his impact can be measured in part by the lack of quality fishing experienced by the average citizen. Frankly, if it were not for the outstanding work performed by fisheries specialists and enforcement officials the situation would be even worse. Ever hear about the good old fishing days when the lakes teemed with large fish? Those stories are true. They might still be true except for the major impact of fish poachers who disregard the laws. That's not to say that everyone who breaks a fishing law is a poacher. Certainly not!

Why do people break fish and game laws? Well, most do not. But of those who do, I believe they do so for three primary reasons: ignorance of the law, being overcome perhaps just once by temptation, and, of course, being a hard core poacher.

First, some people just do not understand the laws or perhaps are unaware of them altogether. And it's the officer's responsibility to assist sportsmen in understanding laws as much as it is to enforce them. Nonetheless, these people still might have to account for their actions, especially if they've harmed the resources. There are very few people who fall into this category, and each officer has to weigh each case on an individual basis.

The second group includes those who know that they are breaking the law but normally would not do so. One such fellow had faithfully bought his fishing license for years. But he had never met a game warden on any of his fishing trips. Within a year and a half he would be at the age where he would no longer be required to have a license. So he figured that this season the odds were in his favor. Because he'd never been checked anyway, he decided not to buy one for the very first time. At least that's what he told the officer who checked him that day.

Or consider the ice fishermen discovered with 30 crappies over his limit. He explained to the officer that for the first time in his life he had finally caught a limit of crappies. He went on to say that the fish were biting so good that temptation overcame him and he just couldn't stop fishing. The conservation officer had walked up just as the angler stepped from his small portable fish house to stretch. On seeing the warden the man quickly climbed back inside. Loud noises of crashing pails and splashing water came from the shelter.

The officer rushed up to the structure and looked inside. The fishermen's arm was down one of the near freezing holes trying to force some of the fish he had caught back down. He was truly embarrassed at his own behavior and took his consequences like a gentleman. There

Minnesota Conservation Officer Dave Rodahl exhibits walleyes and crappies confiscated from poachers. Note the night scope in his hands which enabled him to find the violators in total darkness. Intense enforcement measures are necessary to conserve the resources.

are those like this gentleman who make one time mistakes and will probably never repeat them. Even though he was clearly wrong, it would be pretty hard to refer to this man as a poacher if that was in fact his first and only bad game decision.

The final type of fish or game violator is the hard core poacher. These are the people who presumptuously claim for themselves the right to exploit nature and refuse to share in the responsibility to care for it. There are four basic types of behavior which characterize poachers: they are greedy, they are wasteful, they habitually repeat their violations, and they do not respect wildlife. Most of them will have a combination of two or three of these behaviors to some degree. Some poachers have all four. This can best be illustrated by sharing events from both fish and game poaching cases.

But first let me make an important point. In the many years that I have been a conservation enforcement officer, I have yet to meet a person breaking a conservation law because he was hungry and needed the meat. Surely if an officer does come across such a person he would be treated in a dignified appropriate manner; the average sportsman would want it that way.

GREED AND HABIT

One late summer day one of our officers who was assigned to take calls on the "Turn In Poachers" hot line received a very disturbing complaint. The astonished officer listened in near disbelief as the unknown caller detailed the events of an individual whose greed had reached monumental dimensions. I will assign the fictitious name of Mr. Poacher to the violator to tell this true story.

The concerned caller explained that a party named Mr. Poacher had rented a resort cabin for a few weeks on a central Minnesota lake. He gave the officer the name of the resort and full details of Mr. Poacher's description, including his station wagon's license plate number. He told the officer that the violator lived in one of the major cities of Minnesota and each summer would rent a lake cabin somewhere two or three hours away from home then do nothing but fish.

The caller explained that Mr. Poacher fishes from before sunrise until after the sun sets. He takes a break only long enough to sneak in his catches of fish a limit at a time for his wife to clean. He fishes only for crappies and sunfish which are filleted and packaged in packs of 25 fish each. After about ten days Mr. and Mrs. Poacher will take the fish back to the big city and distribute them. He explained that the fish are never taken to the poacher home, and that there is no way to trace the fish once they reach the cities.

"How many fish are we talking about?" asked the officer. He explained to the caller that in Minnesota an angler is allowed to possess 15 crappies and 30 sunfish, and if his wife fishes she, too, can possess that many. The answer stunned the officer.

"Well over a thousand crappies and sunfish each trip," replied the caller, to which he added, "and he has made four trips already. Look! I'm sick of this going on year after year and I would like to see it stopped. If you send someone into the small town near the resort you will discover that Mr. Poacher has probably rented a locker (small freezer) to store and hide his fish. That's the way he usually operates. But you will have to work fast. He should be preparing to return to the city in the next day or two for the last time this year with a load of fish."

According to the information gathered, Mr. Poacher had already caught over 4,000 crappies and sunfish. His poor wife had to clean them while he fished. Even though it was not she who called to report him, one could not have blamed her after having to clean all those fish if she had done so.

Anyway, the conservation officer, (game warden) in that area was alerted and provided with all the details. The weather had been stormy that week and few boats had dared to go out on the community lakes. But there was at least a chance that Mr. Poacher had caught some fish and would perhaps have too many. Following the proper legal procedures, the officer found the rented locker. It was bulging with packages of fish. He called one of his neighboring wardens to assist him. They would take shifts watching Mr. Poacher and apprehend him after he had picked up the fish.

Within a couple days the fish were picked up to be transported to the city. The wardens stopped the station wagon and explained to Mr. Poacher that they had reason to believe he was over his limit with fish. He was indeed. At first he protested the idea that he had too many fish. He argued that the weather had been so bad that fishing was poorer than normal. One has to wonder what a good fishing trip would have been like for Mr. Poacher since it turned out that he had 760 crappies and 280 sunfish hidden in his station wagon: a total of 1,040 fish!

Mr. Poacher was taken before a judge and in an arrangement with the court agreed to pay a fine of $1,100. He requested that his wife not be told what the fine was. The court agreed and Mr. Poacher counted out 11 one hundred dollar bills to the clerk of court. I think the reader will agree that anyone who can take 11 one hundred dollar bills out of his pocket money without his wife missing it is not poaching out of need but from greed.

Not only was Mr. Poacher greedy, but he repeated his violation time and again. His story is not unique. Remember the man in chapter one who used the pink and yellow jig to take 754 crappies? The citizen who complained about his activities alleges that he had given the man a stern warning the day before for doing the same thing.

Conservation officers in another community arrested four adults for having 1,800 crappies in possession. The sportsman who complained in that situation told the officers that he had knowledge that they had

Conservation Officer Reid Alter (right) assisted by Conservation Officer Steve Jacobson (left) display 1,040 filleted crappies and sunfish confiscated from a greedy fish poacher. Photo courtesy of Officer Jacobson.

done the same thing the year before. And records indicate that one of the individuals in this group had been previously arrested for possessing too many crappies in the same area. One of the arresting officers in that case explained that the 1,800 crappies were caught on feathered jigs.

    One game warden arrived at a resort motel too late one year to apprehend individuals reported to be far over their limit in fish. The officer had the description of the van they were driving, but they had already left the state in an unknown direction by the time of his arrival. For almost a full year the determined officer remembered the van and never passed the motel without checking the parking lot for its return. As luck would have it, the following year that van was back at the motel. The warden's wife, pretending to be the cleaning lady, looked in the motel dumpster and discovered the fresh cleanings of hundreds of fish. Appropriate justice followed.

    Have you ever wondered what happens to all those confiscated fish, rods, reels, or boats? Hardware items like fishing tackle and boats are sold at public auctions, whereas perishable items like fish are usually sold or donated almost immediately. Disabled veteran organizations, charitable groups, and needy persons are at the top of the list to receive

CONSERVATION: A CALL TO STEWARDSHIP

Wardens who 'fried' poachers, fry crappies for elderly

When four out-of-state anglers decided they would catch themselves one big mess of crappies, furnishing the entree for a senior citizens' shindig probably was not what they had in mind.

Local conservation officers, including Duane Lhotka of Aitkin and Jim Bryant of Isle, made last Tuesday a little nicer for more than 150 older Aitkin area residents with a dinner of fresh fried fish. Or should that be poached fish?

Lhotka, Bryant and nine other conservation officers made what Department of Natural Resources officials believe to be the largest confiscation of game fish in Minnesota history in late August in Glen, arresting a husband and wife from Illinois and his parents from Iowa with more crappies than the law allows. About 1800 crappies over the limit.

While the two couples spent their vacation on Elm Island Lake, just west of Glen, officers watched them hook bushel baskets of crappies day after day. Lhotka arrested two of the anglers with over-limits of fish the summer before and suspected they were catching the crappies to sell.

With search warrants in their pockets, two teams of officers stopped the couples in Glen as they left for home before sunrise August 15. In several coolers and a small refrigerator the officers discovered 237 pounds of crappie fillets packed nicely in little plastic bags. It was later estimated the couples had fillets from 1850 fish. The limit is 15 crappies per person.

The four pleaded guilty to charges of fishing over limit and unlawful transportation of filleted game fish, and they received the maximum sentence: fines that totaled $4400, confiscation of their fishing gear worth $2000, including boats and motors, a short stay in the Aitkin County jail and the loss of Minnesota fishing privileges for five years.

And, of course, they also lost the 237 pounds of crappie fillets, which left a lot of tasty evidence to be disposed of by the DNR. Ten officers set up a kitchen on the back lawn of the Aicota Nursing Home on Aitkin's west side, whipped up a beer batter while cooking oil heated in two large fish fryers, and commenced fixing a lunch of fresh crappie for residents of the home and other older guests from the Aitkin area. There was plenty left over to feed the officers and a small group of newspaper, radio and television reporters who stopped by.

Between bites of his second helping of deep-fried crappie, Ed Christian, one of the older guests who came to the nursing home for the lunch, swapped fishing stories with the man seated beside him at one of the extra tables set up in the activity room to accommodate the overflow crowd. He spoke of his preference for catfish, but also said he loved to catch and eat big pike, northerns or walleyes.

"I don't get the chance to go fishing much anymore," Ed said as he poked his fork into another piece of crappie. Steam was still rising from the fillet. And in the background was a polka being played by a man seated at an organ, accompanied by another who played trumpet and doubled on saxophone.

Ed wore a big smile along with his light blue jacket and bola tie around his neck. "This sure is delicious," he said.

Ed Christian, Aitkin, enjoyed the meal.

Photographs and story by Mike Gustafson

Conservation officer Duane Lhotka, Aitkin, removed a crappie fillet from the fryer.

Officers cooking outdoors passed the fish through a window to Helen Swedberg, who served it to residents and guests.

Tending to one fish fryer was officer Jim Bryant, Isle.

Officers who worked on the case in which the fish were seized were cooks.

This article which appeared in the **Mille Lacs Messenger,** a Minnesota newspaper, is indicative of many such events conducted by Conservation Officers (game wardens) nationwide. Here, officers have donated over 200 pounds of confiscated crappies to serve over 150 senior citizens a fish fry treat. (Reprinted with permission).

WASTE AND DISRESPECT FOR THE CREATURE

A sense of indignation always returns as I recall walking up on a particular fisherman one day whose behavior certainly illustrates the abuses of both waste and disrespect. As I was approaching he caught a couple of crappies which he felt were too small. Instead of gently releasing them he slammed them against some rocks along the rivers edge. Angrily I asked him why he would do such a thing. His only explanation was that the fish were too small so he didn't think it was any big deal.

While it's not a fishing story, consider the report from one officer who was watching deer on a field one night. The deer were grazing near a road. Unaware of the officer's presence, someone drove a truck slowly by shining the field with a spotlight. On spotting the deer, the driver slammed on the brakes, stuck a gun out the window, and shot one of the animals. The vehicle then raced away with the offender

Evidence of waste and disrespect for nature: Every winter scenes like this are common on some lakes.

never intending to pick up the dead deer. As he drove off, he screamed out the window, "Die, Bucky! Die!" When apprehended he had no explanation for his wasteful action.

The previous examples are fairly obvious acts of unsportsmanlike waste and certainly reveal the perpetrators, disrespect for the value of wildlife. But sometimes the acts are more subtle. Aside from their plainly blatant selfishness, think of the impact of those who sneak into the streams each spring to illegally net and spear the less prolific species which are trying to spawn. Surely these finny creatures have a right to spawn and that right should be respected, but it isn't. Billions of fish will never exist to be caught in their season by honest anglers because roe-filled fish are gored and hauled off in poachers' sacks.

It is my hope that the foregoing examples have convinced the reader that those who over-harvest and abuse the resources are doing so not from ignorance or need, but from choice. Their basic problem is one of attitude. Rarely will you meet anyone these days that does not understand the importance of the principles of conservation. But knowing and doing are really two different things.

The majority of fishermen and hunters never deliberately break conservation laws. If fact, it is due to their concern and insistence that many states have developed nongovernmental, sportsman-sponsored programs set up to combat the abuses of poachers.

These programs provide a toll-free phone service which allows citizens from anywhere in the state to anonymously report fish or game violations. In fact-many of the programs present rewards to the unknown caller if the information leads to the arrest of the violators.

In Minnesota where I serve as a conservation officer the program is known as **TURN IN POACHERS.** It is funded entirely by private contributions from citizens and administered by a board of directors who are elected by contributing members. These programs have been outstanding successes because of the involvement of supportive sportsmen.

HABITAT ABUSE: TROUBLED WATERS

Poaching is by no means the only negative force to contend with which threatens the future of quality fishing. The life giving rivers and lakes are slowly dying (or are being killed). For example, while checking fishermen along the banks of the beautiful and once pristine Saint Croix River one officer was actually sickened by the results of an event which took place only moments before his arrival. A fishermen and his wife were taking up their lines to stop fishing. On seeing the officer the gentleman pointed at the river and angrily asked "Can't you do something about that?"

A large commercial boat was docked just a few feet from where the angler had been fishing. Swirling about the boat was evidence of large quantities of human waste. According to facts gathered by the officer, the boat had just discharged 400 gallons of raw human sewage into the river. The boat captain was given a citation, pled guilty, and fined. However distasteful and ruinous, such overt acts do not compare to the sinister long term damaging effects of acid rain and other subtle forms of industrial pollution. And at an alarming rate, increasing numbers of states are issuing advisories warning the public against eating too much of some types of fish which have been contaminated by polluted waters.

Interestingly, the claspingleaf pondweed for which crappies have such a fondness will only grow in water that is relatively pollution free. The crappies' preference for this pure water plant should be instructive. It certainly suggests a continued need for action to protect our waters for the salvation of the future of fishing.

Could the genetic defect on this otherwise apparently healthy crappie be due to pollution?

As I consider the approaching concerns for the environment, I am reminded of the poetic words of the ancient Psalmist who first wrote, "O Lord, how manifold are thy works! In wisdom thou hast made them all; the earth is full of thy creatures. Yonder is the sea, great and wide, which teems with things innumerable, living things both small and great." Then after several lines of thankful praises wishfully adds, "May the glory of the Lord endure forever, may the Lord rejoice in his works."

Will these "works" endure? Or will our great rivers which teem with life become sewer ditches? Will our lakes and ponds be forever poisoned? Respect and care will be achieved only through conviction and knowledge. The true sportsman must avail himself of every opportunity to study these issues and work to see that this doesn't happen. The crappie's habitat is a complex ecological system worthy of the greatest respect and care possible. Disregard for conservation principles and the pollution of our waters are not only the two greatest threats to our fishing, but threatens our own well being as well.

Quality angling now and in the future depends just as much upon continued application of conservation ethics as surely as knowing the secrets of fishing lures and good fishing holes. I wish to thank the reader for the opportunity to share the many ideas presented. Good luck fishing and I hope to meet you on the water.

The smile of this small child is a rewarding reminder of the need for conservation officials and sportsmen to continue to work together to insure the future of quality fishing.

APPENDIX A
FINDING SUPPLIES FOR MAKING JIGS

Most well stocked-sports shops which include fishing equipment will have most items you will need for tying your own jigs. But you can save money by buying large quantities from any of the following mail order places. Each will send you a free catalog just for the asking.

Cabela's
812 -13th Ave
Sidney, NB 69160

Everything needed. Catalog available.

Component Systems
5003 Packer Drive
Wausau, WI
54401 Phone (715) 845-3009

The best jig paints available. Unpainted jigs in all sizes. Catalog available.

Tackle-Craft
P.O. Box 280
Chippewa Falls, WI
54729

Everything needed. Catalog available.

APPENDIX B
HOW TO BUILD A FLY TYING VISE FOR UNDER A DOLLAR

You can assemble a very inexpensive fly (jig) tying vise in about 10 minutes from just a few items you might already have around the house. Following is a list of items needed:

1) One six-inch long 4x4 block of wood. Two six-inch lengths of 2x4 nailed together will do.
2) One 13-inch long 1x2 board. Drill a ¼ inch hole in one end of the 1x2 to accommodate a ¼ inch bolt.
3) Two standard ¼ inch nuts.
4) One ¼ inch bolt which is 3 inches long.
5) Two ¼ washers.
6) One ¼ inch wing nut.
7) Two ¼ inch screws.

Assemble these parts as shown in the illustration.

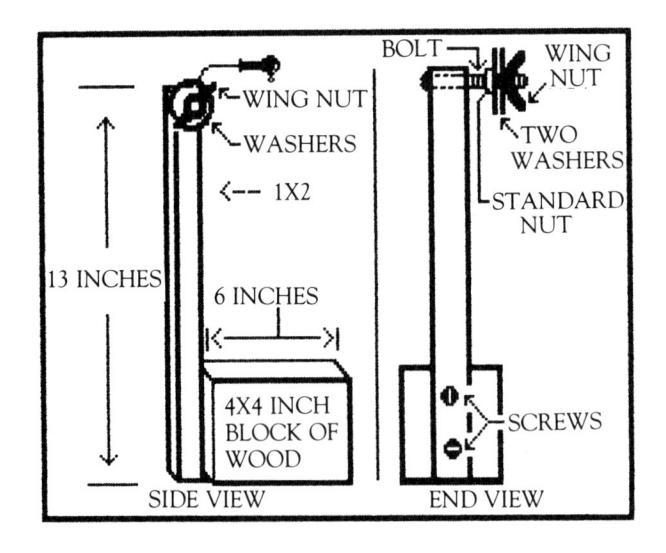

APPENDIX C
MAKING A MARKER BUOY

Marker buoys are very useful tools which allow an angler to hold his/her position over a hump or on a point where fish have been located. Because buoys are easily broken it can become costly to continuously replace them. However, excellent buoys can be made for next to nothing in just a few easy steps.

Take a six inch by four inch piece of styrofoam which is approximately two inches thick. Lay the sheet of styrofoam on a flat surface and cut away sections from the sides. The results should look like the capital letter I as illustrated. Next tie a 20 to 30 feet length of discarded fly line or 50 lb. test braided line to the center of the I. After winding the entire length of the line around the styrofoam, attach three one-ounce lead bell sinkers to the end of the line. That's all there is to it.

When you are over a spot that you would like to mark, just drop the buoy overboard. The weights will plummet to the bottom and the flat longer ends of the buoy will prevent it from turning over from the wind. Otherwise the buoy could move as far downwind as the extra line would permit and thereby not remain over the target area.

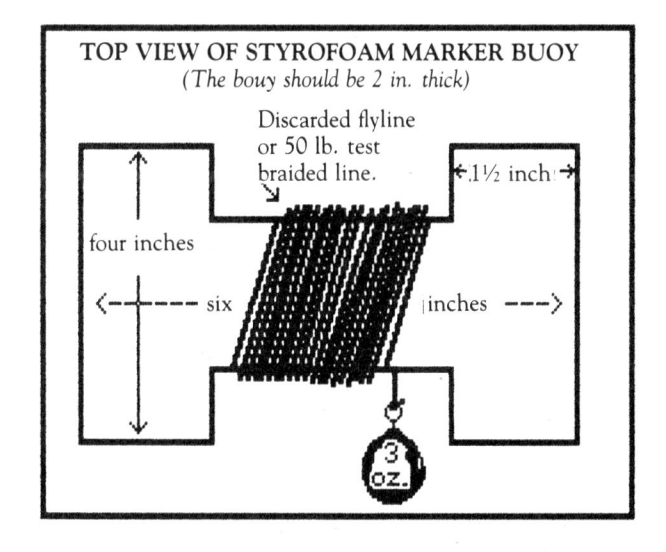

TOP VIEW OF STYROFOAM MARKER BUOY
(The bouy should be 2 in. thick)

THE AUTHOR

Wayne Eller, serves as a natural resource Conservation Officer (Game Warden) with the state of Minnesota, the land of 10,000 lakes. From a lifetime of fishing experiences and years of study, the author has refined crappie angling techniques to an art. The ideas presented were derived from thousands of crappies caught (and released), and years of observing anglers both as a hobby and a profession. Wayne's other interests include giving fishing lectures and workshops, fly tying, outdoor photography, and flying.

He attended Bethel College in St. Paul and the University of Minnesota. Originally from South Carolina, home of the world record black crappie, he brings the best ideas from both North and South to this book.

THE BOOK

This splendid guide to crappie fishing has 47 full color photographs, 38 computer assisted illustrations, and other features aimed at helping anglers catch crappies. It was designed as an instructional handbook in an easy-to-read style to be informative and appealing to anglers of every experience level.

Features
- Natural history of white and black crappies.
- Walleye, bass, and other gamefish tips are included.
- The effect of weather conditions on successful crappie fishing.
- The best crappie lures based on biological responses and habitat.
- Fly tying instructions for the most effective crappie catching jigs.
- How to fish ice out crappies in canals, bays, culverts, and streams.
- How to find and catch crappies under floating cattail bogs, water hyacinths, and other shaded structures.
- Reed fishing.
- Fishing flooded timber from small ponds to reservoirs, beaver lodges, cypress tree roots, creek channels, and timber spawning areas.
- The crappie's favored aquatic plants. Post spawn and summer hideouts.
- River and stream crappies.
- Ice fishing. How to find crappie sanctuaries in the winter.
- Game violations. A frank discussion on why it happens and its impact.